Using EViews For

Mark A. Reiman
Pacific Lutheran University

R. Carter Hill
Louisiana State University

UNDERGRADUATE ECONOMETRICS
Second Edition

R. Carter Hill
Louisiana State University

William E. Griffiths
University of New England, Australia

George G. Judge
University of California Berkeley

John Wiley & Sons, Inc.

New York • Chichester • Weinheim • Brisbane • Singapore • Toronto

To order books or for customer service call 1-800-CALL-WILEY (225-5945).

ISBN 0-471-41239-2

Printed in the United States of America

10 9 8 7 6 5 4 3 2

Printed and bound by Victor Graphics, Inc.

Contents

Preface

This book is a supplement to *Undergraduate Econometrics, 2nd Edition* by Carter Hill, Bill Griffiths and George Judge (Wiley, 2001), hereinafter *UE/2*. We show you how to perform the computations, step by step, in each chapter of that book using EViews econometric software. Consequently, this book will be useful to students taking econometrics, as well as their instructors, and others who wish to use EViews for econometric analysis. We have tried to include in this book all the material we would like our students to have at their fingertips as they read *UE/2* and work on the exercises therein.

EViews is a very powerful program that is easy to use for data management, statistical analysis, creating graphs, and printing results. To learn more about EViews, visit their website at **http://www.eviews.com**. Output from EViews is easily incorporated into documents, simplifying report writing.

In addition to supporting EViews, the authors of *UE/2* also provide support for the computer software packages SAS, SHAZAM and Excel. To find out more about these supplements visit their web site, **http://www.wiley.com/college/hill**. There the reader will also find all the data files used in *UE/2*, as well as other resources for students and instructors.

The chapters in this book parallel the chapters in *UE/2*. Thus if you seek help for the examples in Chapter 11 of the textbook, check Chapter 11 in this book.

We welcome comments about this book, and suggestions for improvements.

Mark A. Reiman
Department of Economics
Pacific Lutheran University
Tacoma, WA 98447
reimanma@plu.edu

R. Carter Hill
Economics Department
Louisiana State University
Baton Rouge, LA 70803
eohill@lsu.edu

EViews Workfiles Created in <u>Using EViews for Undergraduate Econometrics</u>, 2nd Edition

Chapter 1:   demo.wfl
Chapter 3:   table3_1.wfl
Chapter 4:   table3_1.wfl
Chapter 5:   table3_1.wfl
Chapter 6:   table3_1.wfl
                    wa-wheat.wfl
Chapter 7:   hamburger.wfl
Chapter 8:   hamburger.wfl
                    chap8-3.wfl
                    beer.wfl
Chapter 9:   utown.wfl
                    invest.wfl
Chapter 10:   pizza.wfl
                    nonlin.wfl
                    steel.wfl
                    keepit.wfl
Chapter 11:   foodexp.wfl
                    wheat.wfl
Chapter 12:   sugar.wfl
Chapter 13:   table13-1.wfl
                    table13-2.wfl
Chapter 14:   truffles.wfl
Chapter 15:   capexp.wfl
Chapter 16:   fig16_1.wfl
                    fig16_2.wfl
Chapter 17:   invest1.wfl
                    invest2.wfl
Chapter 18:   transport.wfl

Chapter 1 Introduction to EViews

In this introductory chapter we present the basics of EViews, Version 3.1. In subsequent chapters we will lead you through the use of EViews to complete the examples in *Undergraduate Econometrics*, *2nd Edition*, by Hill, Griffiths and Judge (John Wiley & Sons, Inc., 2001), which we will abbreviate as *UE/2*.

1.1 Creating a Workfile

Your first step in EViews will be to create a workfile. One way to create a workfile is to click **File/New/Workfile**.

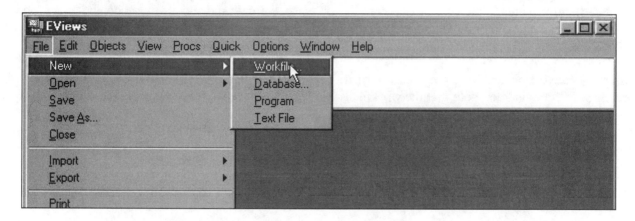

Enter the frequency of the data and the starting and stopping dates. In the example below we are using cross-sectional data, which consist of 40 undated observations. Click on **Undated or irregular** in the workfile frequency. Enter 1 as **start observation** and 40 as **end observation**.

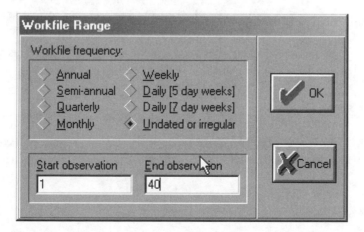

Note: This feature of EViews means that you MUST look at the data file before you try to import it.

1

The rules for describing calendar or ordered data are:

- Annual: specify the year; for example, 1981, 1895, 382, or 95. Years in the 21st and subsequent centuries must be identified with full-year identifiers (e.g. 2020 or 9789 or 50234). Years prior to the 20th century must also be identified with full identifiers (e.g. 382 or 1776 or 1492). Years in the 20th century may be identified using either 2 or 4-digit identifiers (e.g. 97 or 1997). Note that because 2-digit identifiers are assumed to be in the 20th century, EViews cannot handle dates prior to A.D. 100.
- Quarterly: the year, followed by a colon or period, and the quarter number. Examples: 1992:1, 65:4, 2002:3, 1952.1, 1996.4.
- Monthly: the year, followed by a colon or period, and the month number. Examples: 1956:1, 1990:11.
- Weekly and daily: by default, you should specify these dates as month number, followed by a colon, followed by the day number, followed by a colon, followed by the year. Using the **Options/Dates-Frequency** menu item, you can reverse the order of the day and month by switching to European notation. For example, entering 8:10:97 indicates that you want your workfile to begin with August 10, 1997.

After you have finished supplying the information about the type of workfile and clicked OK, you will see the workfile window. Note that the workfile is UNTITLED since we have not yet saved the workfile.

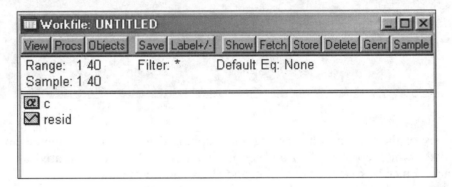

There are two icons in this newly created workfile. These icons represent the objects that are contained in every workfile: a vector of coefficients, C, and a series of residuals, RESID. The little icon to the left identifies the type of object, an α for a coefficient vector and a tiny time series plot for a series. The purpose of these two objects will be explained later.

1.2   Importing a Text (ASCII) Data File

To import data, which is either a text (ascii) file, a Lotus *.wks file or an Excel *.xls file, click on **File/Import/Read Text-Lotus-Excel**. In this case we are going to import an ascii file called *table3-1.dat*.

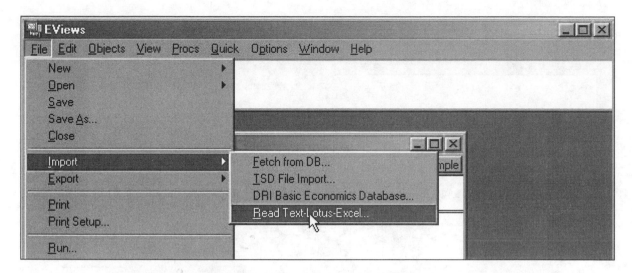

Use the dialog box to locate and select the file you want. Click on **Open**.

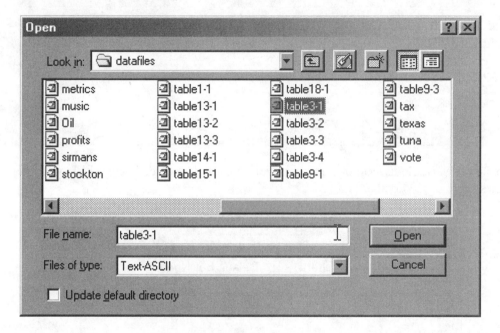

A dialog box will open, which is shown on the next page. If the data file has variable names in the first row, you simply indicate how many series there are. If the data file does not have names, enter them as shown. **<u>Again we note that you must look at the data file before trying to import data.</u>** We are importing 2 variables, *y* and *x*. Note at the bottom of the dialog box the first few observations in the data file are shown.

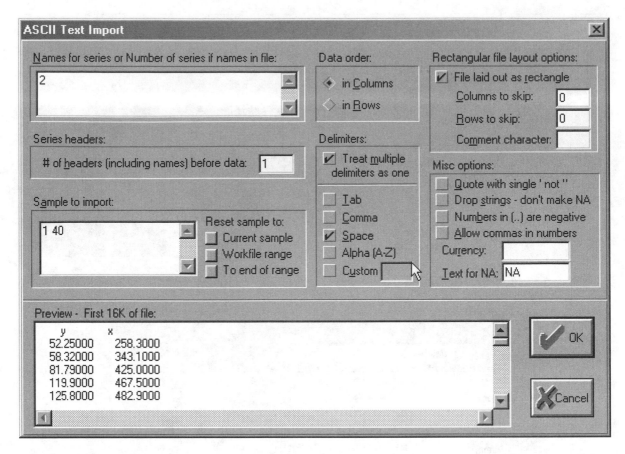

Click **OK** once the variable names, or number of variables, are entered. The workfile will then show that two new series have been added, *x* and *y*.

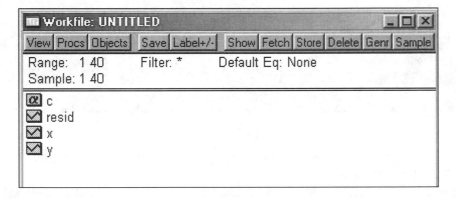

Before proceeding, let us save the workfile. By saving it we will be able to recall it whenever we want, and it will contain all the information (objects) we have added to it.

Click on the **Save** button on the workfile toolbar, and the dialog box shown on the next page will open.

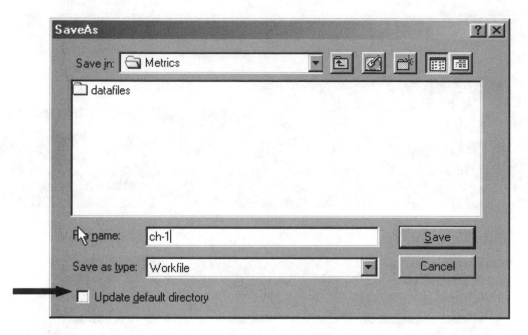

Type in the name for the workfile and use the SAVE IN window to find the directory you want to use. Then click on **Save**.

Note: To change the "**default directory**," click on the box in the lower left hand corner, indicated by the arrow above. EViews will look in the selected directory for files, etc., unless told otherwise.

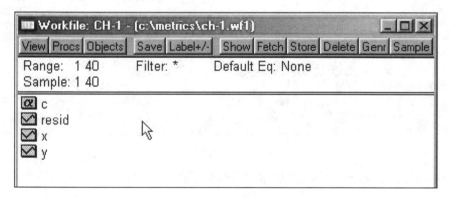

The workfile will now be named, and the path shown at the top of the EViews window. All workfiles are given the extension *.wf1 by EViews.

You are now ready to work with the data in the workfile you have created, or you can close this file and move on to something else returning later to re-open this work file. To open an EViews workfile, click **File/Open/Workfile**

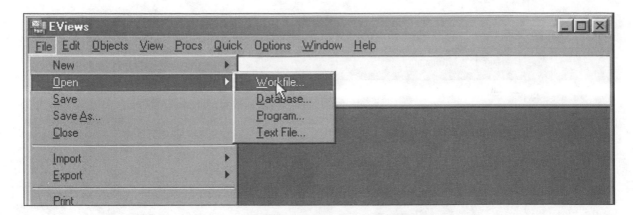

A dialog box opens in which you can select a workfile.

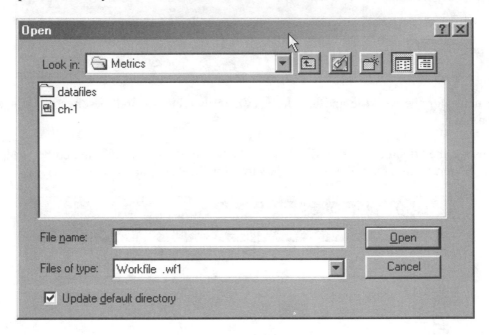

1.3   *Importing Data Contained in an Excel File*

Importing Excel or Lotus spreadsheets use the same steps. Select **File/New/Workfile**. Here we will import quarterly data from 1952.1 to 1996.4 from a file called *demo.xls*. This file is available at the *UE/2* web site, **http://www.wiley.com/college/hill**. We have already opened this Excel file to see its contents, as you should do.

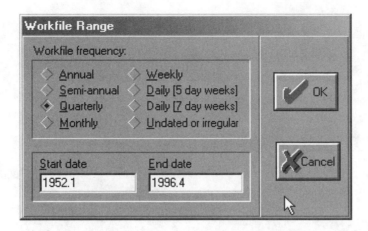

Once the UNTITLED workfile opens, select **File/Import/Read Text-Lotus-Excel**. Select the file type to be Excel .xls and click on the Excel file you want to import.

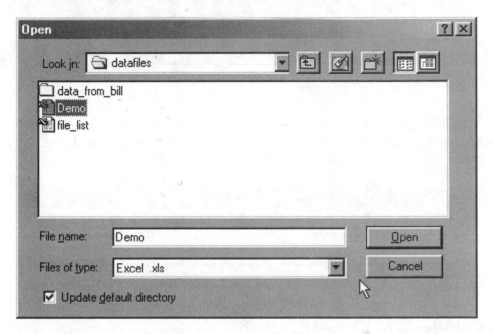

This Excel file has 4 variables, with the first row containing variable names. Note that the upper-left data cell is specified to be B2, since we do not have to import the column containing the dates.

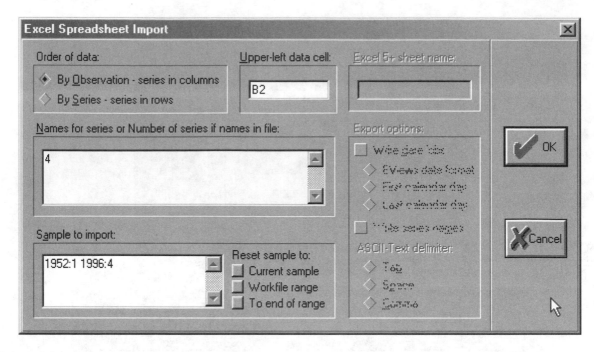

Click **OK**.

The workfile will now contain the data series from the spreadsheet, with icons representing each of the series. Note that below the tabs in the workfile the Range and Sample are set to the limits of the data. The use of Range and Sample will be discussed later.

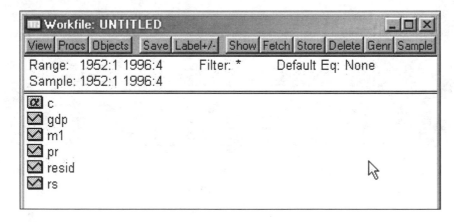

Now you are ready to save this workfile (name it *demo*), and then work with it.

1.4   Entering Data Manually

Most of the time you will import data which are in a text file or an Excel file. However, for small problems, you can enter data directly into EViews.

As always, you must first create a workfile. Just to illustrate the process, we will create a workfile containing 2 series of 4 observations, named *y* and *x*.

Click on **File/New/Workfile**.

We will assume we have annual observations, from 1996 to 1999. Click **OK**. This will open a workfile.

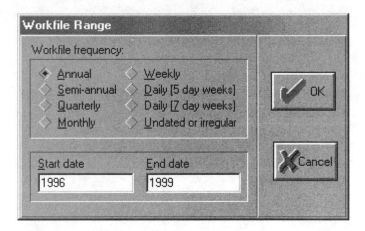

Select **Quick/Empty Group (Edit Series)**.

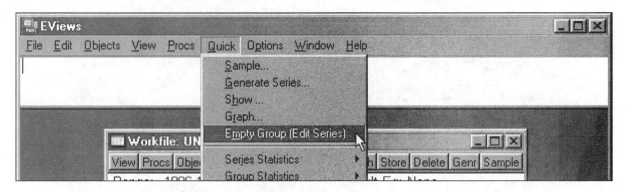

A spreadsheet will open in which you can enter your data.

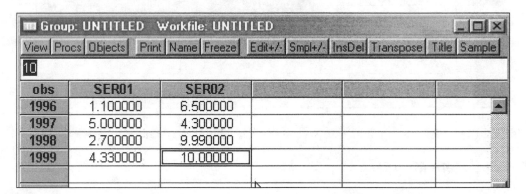

As you fill in the data, EViews will assign temporary names, **SER01** and **SER02**, to the variables. To change those names do the following:

- Highlight column 1 by clicking on the name **SER01.**
- On the command line type **x** and hit **enter**.
- A dialog box, shown on the next page, will appear asking you to confirm the name change. Click **Yes**.

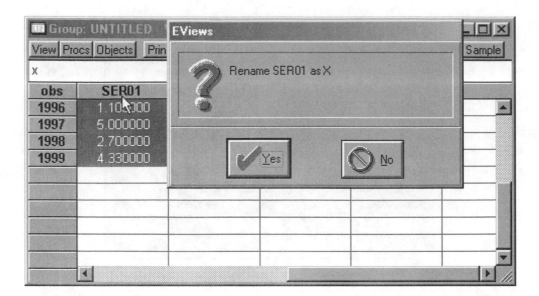

Repeat the process for the second column. Close the spreadsheet by clicking on the "**x**" in the upper right hand corner. You will be asked if you want to delete the **GROUP**. We will discuss GROUPs later. For now, delete the GROUP.

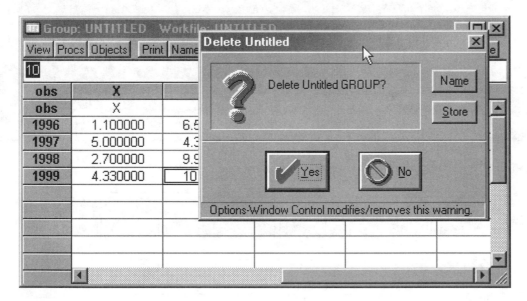

You should find the series *x* and *y* added to your workfile, which you then **save**.

1.5   EViews Help Menu

Should you forget how to do something, EViews has excellent online **HELP**. Click on **Help/EViews Help Topics.**

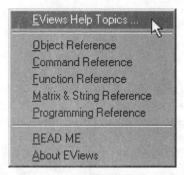

A drop down menu appears Double Click on **EViews Basics**.

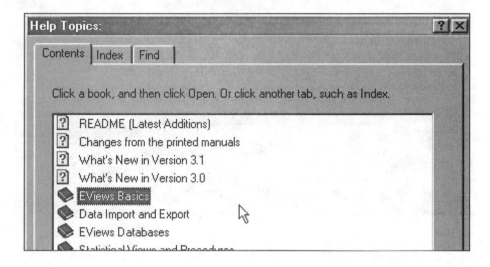

Up pops a list of topics from which you can choose.

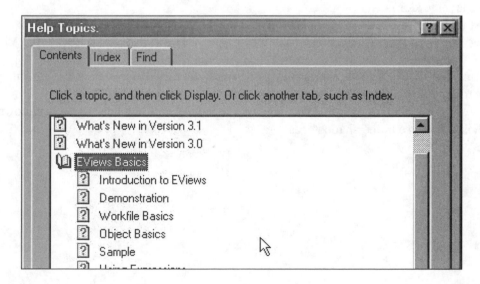

You are encouraged to explore these, although many times you will find more information than you wanted to know. A little searching may be required to find the answer to the question you have.

See the help section **Data Import and Export** for more on the topics covered in Chapter 1.1-1.5.

1.6 Examining the Data

Open the workfile called *demo* by clicking **File/Open/Workfile** and selecting demo.

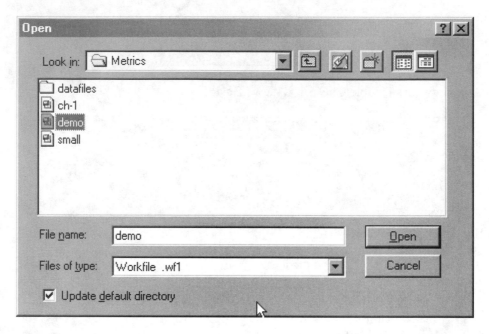

In this workfile the variables are:
- GDP—gross domestic product
- M1—money supply
- PR—price level (index)
- RS—short term interest rate

When examining the data the first task is always to verify that the desired data have been imported. To look at one or more series in the workfile,
- select the series you wish to examine by dragging the mouse, with the left button held down,
- double-click anywhere in the shaded area

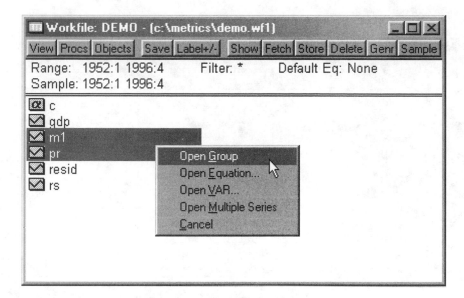

Click on **Open Group**. A spreadsheet view of the data will open. Compare these data values to those in the original file, to make sure the data have been properly imported.

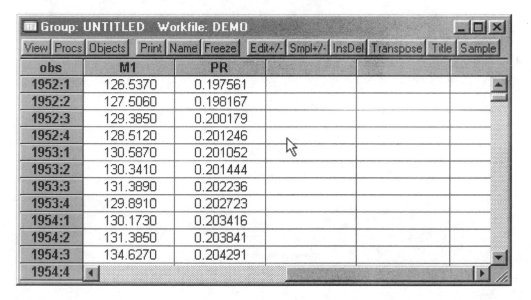

1.7   Plotting the Data

We can plot the data in several ways. One way is from the spreadsheet view above. The other is using **Quick/Graph**.

1.7.1 Plotting from the Spreadsheet View

Keep this group window open to examine graphs of M1 and PR for these two variables.

EViews allows you to easily construct a variety of plots of the data. In the GROUP window above, click on **View/Multiple Graphs/Line**. By choosing **Multiple Graphs** each variable will be plotted in a separate graph. Choosing **Graph** would have produced a single plot containing both series, which is uninformative here because the variables are of such different scales.

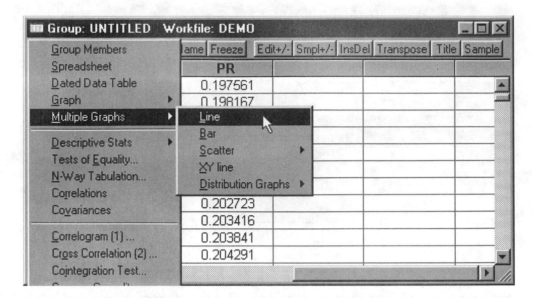

The vertical axis gives the value of the series at each time point, which is plotted on the horizontal axis.

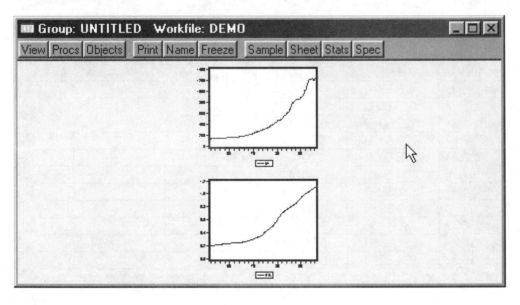

These plots can be printed by clicking on **Print** on the tool bar. Close the plots by clicking on the "**x**" in the upper right-hand corner. Answer "**yes**" to query about deleting untitled GROUP.

1.7.2   Plotting using **Quick/Graph**

Plots of any variables in the workfile can be created another way. In the workfile window, click on **Quick/Graph**.

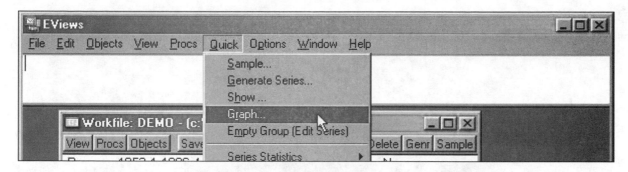

A dialog box opens asking which series you would like plotted. Let us look at GDP.

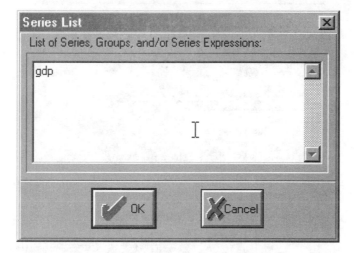

You are then asked what type of graph you would like.

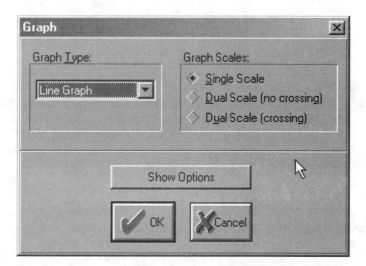

If you click **OK**, you will obtain a line graph like those of M1 and PR. In the graph window, click the **x** in the upper right hand corner.

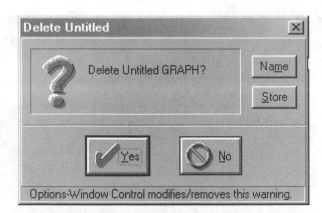

Do you want to save this graph? Click on **Name** and type in the name **gdp_plot**.

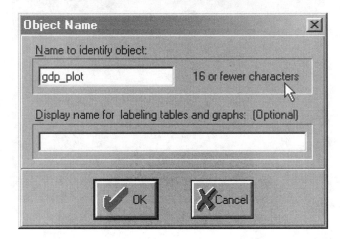

Click **OK**. You will find an icon in the workfile window named **gdp_plot**. If you double click this icon up will pop the graph of GDP.

The EViews help file contains extensive information about altering the characteristics of the plot, adding text, etc. Click on **Help/Index**. Type in **Graph/Display**. Scroll down the list to find **Working with Graphs**. Click **Display**. An extensive description of working with graphs will be displayed.

1.7.3   Copying Graphs into Documents

You can incorporate an EViews graph directly into a document in your Windows word processor. To do this, first activate the object window containing the graph you wish to move; click anywhere in the window so that the titlebar changes to a bright color. Then click **Edit/Copy** on the EViews main menu.

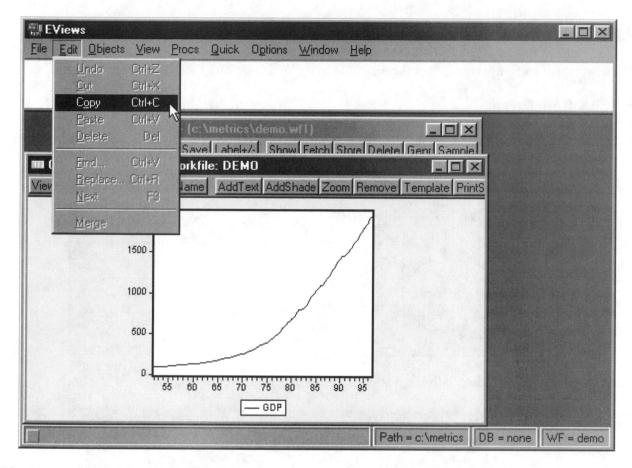

The Copy Graph as Metafile dialog box appears.

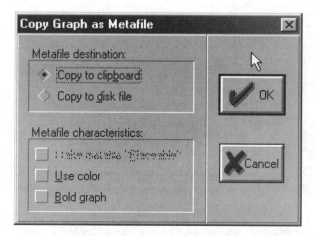

You can copy the graph to the Windows clipboard or to a disk file. You can request that the graph be in color and that its lines be in bold. Copy graphs in black-and-white unless you will be printing to a color printer.

If you copy a graph to the clipboard, you can switch to your word processor and paste the graph into your document. Standard programs such as Word or WordPerfect will give you a graph that can be sized, positioned, and modified within the program. Try this now.

1.8   Descriptive Statistics

In the workfile *demo*, again highlight the series M1 and PR, then double click in the shaded area.

- Click **Open Group**.
- Click the **View** button on the toolbar.
- Click **Descriptive Stats/Common Sample**. The choice between **Common Sample** and **Individual Samples** does not matter, except when a series has missing values.

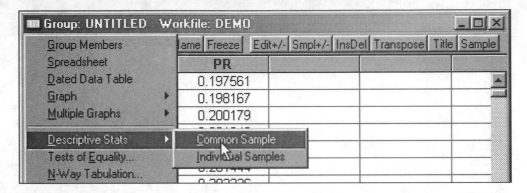

This produces a table of descriptive statistics for the two variables in the group.

	M1	PR			
Mean	445.0064	0.514106			
Median	298.3990	0.383802			
Maximum	1219.420	1.110511			
Minimum	126.5370	0.197561			
Std. Dev.	344.8315	0.303483			
Skewness	0.997776	0.592712			
Kurtosis	2.687096	1.829239			
Jarque-Bera	30.60101	20.81933			
Probability	0.000000	0.000030			

The definitions of these summary measures, and their formulas, are found in the Help menu—**Help/EViews Help Topics/Statistical Views and Procedures/Series Views**.

The values of these summary statistics can be printed, by clicking the **Print** button. Alternatively, the values can be transferred to a document by highlighting the column(s) you want to copy, click **Edit/Copy** and how you want the copy to be done. Switch to your word processor and paste in the values, which appear as a table, which can be further edited.

While viewing the descriptive statistics, click on **View**. The drop-down menu shows a variety of statistical measures and tables you can obtain for the two variables in the group, such as **Correlations** and **Covariances**, as well as more advanced measures and tests.

1.9   Histograms

Another important view of the data is provided by a **Histogram**, which shows the distribution of the values of a series. In the workfile, select a **single series**, say M1. Double click in the shaded area. A spreadsheet view of the single series will appear. Select **View/Descriptive Statistics/Histogram and Stats**.

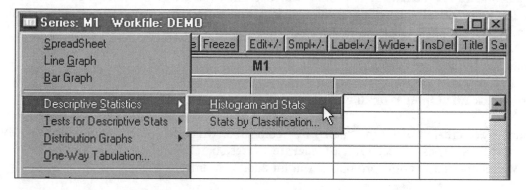

Which produces

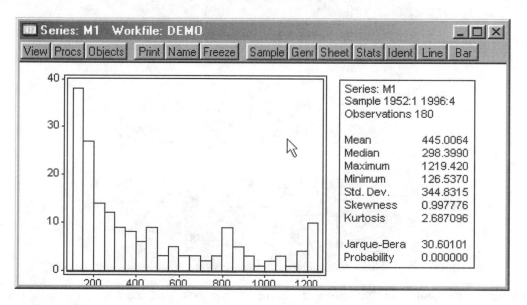

Print the histogram and summary statistics for M1 by clicking the **Print** button on the toolbar. You can incorporate the histogram directly into a document. Click anywhere in the window so that the titlebar changes to a bright color. Then click **Edit/Copy** on the EViews main menu. If you copy a graph to the clipboard, you can switch to your word processor and paste the graph into your document. See **Working with Graphs** in the Help menu for instructions on how to edit the graph, add titles, etc.

1.10   Creating and Deleting Variables

One of the most powerful features of EViews is the ability to use and to process mathematical expressions. EViews contains an extensive library of built-in operators and functions that allow you to perform complicated mathematical operations on your data with just a few keystrokes. In addition to supporting standard mathematical and statistical operations, EViews provides a number of specialized functions for automatically handling the leads, lags and differences that are commonly found in time series data.

To illustrate , open the saved workfile DEMO.

- Click **File/Open/Workfile**. Using the dialog box, select **Demo**.

New variables are created using the **"generate"** command, which is abbreviated as **Genr** in EViews. To create or modify a series, select **Quick/Generate Series,** or click on the **Genr** button on the workfile toolbar. EViews opens a window prompting you for additional information.

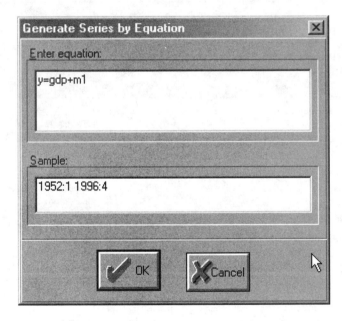

You should enter the assignment statement in the upper edit box, and the relevant sample period in the lower edit box. In the open dialog window type **y = gdp + m1**. Click **OK**. You will see that the variable *y* now appears in the workfile. The lower window shows the sample range used for the calculation.

Alternatively, type **genr y = gdp + m1** in the EViews command window and hit enter. The variable **y = gdp + m1** is not of interest. To delete it, locate the **Objects** button on the Workfile toolbar. Select (highlight) *y*, then

Click **Objects/Delete selected/Yes**

1.11   The Basic Mathematical Operations

The basic mathematical operators are

Expression	Operator	Description
+	add	x+y adds the contents of X and Y
−	subtract	x−y subtracts the contents of Y from X
*	multiply	x*y multiplies the contents of X by Y
/	divide	x/y divides the contents of X by Y
^	raise to the power	x^y raises X to the power of Y

All of these operators may be used in expressions involving series and scalar values. When applied to a series expression, the operation is performed for each observation in the current sample.

In more complicated expressions there is always a question of the **order of computations**. For example, what is computed by the expression

genr y = −3 + 2 * 4

Is y = −4 (which is −3 + 2 = −1 times 4) or is y = 5 (which is 2 times 4 added to minus 3)? The answer is y = 5.

EViews follows the usual order in evaluating expressions from <u>left to right</u>, with operator precedence order (from highest precedence to lowest):

- The signs minus (-), and plus (+)
- ^ (exponentiation)
- *, / (multiplication and division)
- +, - (addition and subtraction)

To enforce a particular order of evaluation, you can use parentheses. As in standard mathematical analysis, terms which are enclosed in parentheses are evaluated first, from the innermost to the outermost set of parentheses. We strongly recommend the use of parentheses when there is any possibility of ambiguity in your expression.

genr y = (−3 + 2) * 4 equals −4.
genr y = −3 + (2 * 4) equals 5.

1.12   Using EViews Functions

EViews contains an extensive library of built-in functions that operate on all of the elements of a series in the current sample. Some of the functions are "element functions" which return a value for each element of the series, while others are "summary functions" which return scalars, vectors or matrices, which may then be used in constructing new series. To view the entire list, click **Help/Function Reference**.

Most function names in EViews are preceded by the **@**-sign. For example, **@mean** returns the average value of a series taken over the current sample, and **@abs** takes the absolute value of each observation in the current sample.

To illustrate the difference

> Click **Genr**. Enter the equation y = log(gdp). Click **OK**.
> Click **Genr**. Enter the equation z = @mean(gdp). Click **OK**.

Highlight y. **Double-click** the shaded area.   The values of y are the natural logarithm for each value of **gdp** in the sample.

Highlight z. **Double-click** the shaded area. The value of $z = 632.4190$, which is the average of the sample **gdp** values. This number is repeated for each observation in the sample because the function **@mean** returns a single value, or scalar.

1.13 Creating Coefficient Vectors

The equation **z = @mean(gdp)** creates a variable all of whose values are the same. Sometimes this is useful. However it may also be useful to store the single number in a **coefficient** vector.

A coefficient vector can be created by typing **coef(*n*) coef_name** in the command line. The value n is the length of the coefficient vector and the number of constants which can be stored. If (*n*) is omitted a vector of length 1 is created, which can hold a single, scalar, value. The *coef_name* is the name of the coefficient vector that will appear in the workfile.

For example, in the EViews command window, type **coef(10) result** and hit enter. The icon α **RESULT**,

α result

appears in the workfile. Highlight **result, double-click** the shaded area. You see the series with elements **R1-R10**, all of which are initially zeros. This coefficient vector is a storage bin into which we can place numbers for future use.

Alternatively, click **Objects/New Object/ Matrix-Vector-Coef**. Type in a name for the object and click **OK**. Click **Coefficient Vector**. Enter the desired number of rows and click **OK**.

The coefficient vector elements are created using the **genr** command. On the workfile toolbar click the **genr** button. Type

> result(1) = @mean(gdp). Click **OK**.
> Highlight **result, double-click** the shaded area. Note that R1= 632.4190.

Once stored the elements of the coefficient vector can be used in further calculations. For example, to compute the sample mean squared,

> Click the **genr** button.
> Type result(2) = (result(1))^2. Click **OK**.

Or, to create a new variable, say **gdpstar**, which is **gdp** divided by its sample mean,

> Click the **genr** button.

Type gdpstar = gdp/result(1). Click **OK**.

A coefficient vector can be printed several ways.

(a)   In the workfile window, highlight **result**. Click **View/Print Selected**.

(b)   Highlight **result**, **double-click** the shaded area. Click the **Print** button on the toolbar.

(c)   Highlight **result**, **double-click** the shaded area.   Click on **C1**, which highlights the column. Enter **Ctrl/C** (while pressing **Ctrl** type **C**) to copy the column into the Windows clipboard.   Switch to your word processor, enter **Ctrl/V** to paste the column into your document as a table. You may then edit the table in the usual way.

Chapter 2 Computing Normal Probabilities

2.1 *Cumulative Normal Probabilities*

The EViews function **@cnorm(z)** returns the cumulative probability that a standard normal random variable falls to the left of the given value **z**, as illustrated below.

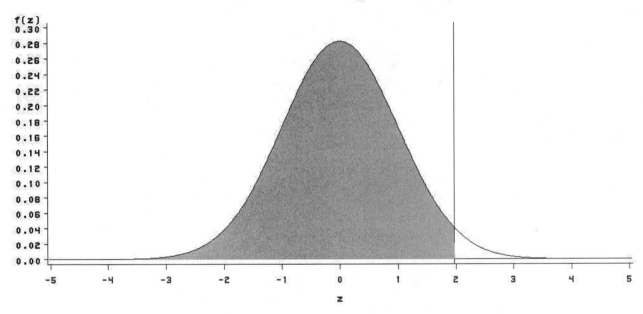

A Cumulative Probability
Shaded Area is P(Z< = 1.96)

- Click on **File/New/Workfile**
- Click on **Undated**. Enter some number for observations, say 10, though is doesn't matter here since we will not be entering data. Click **OK**.
- Create a storage vector in which to save calculations. Click **Objects/New Object/Matrix-Vector-Coef**. Enter a name for the object, say **normprob**. Click **OK**.

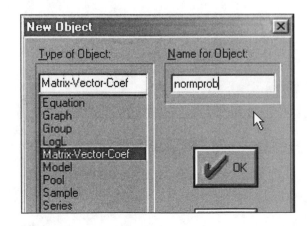

- In the "New Matrix" dialog box, click **Coefficient Vector**.   Enter a number of rows, such as 10.
  Click **OK**.
-

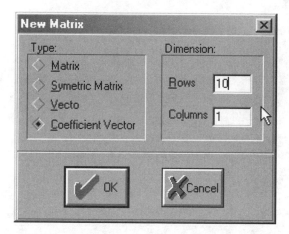

A blank spread sheet will appear, which is the vector **normprob**, with 10 rows and 1 column.

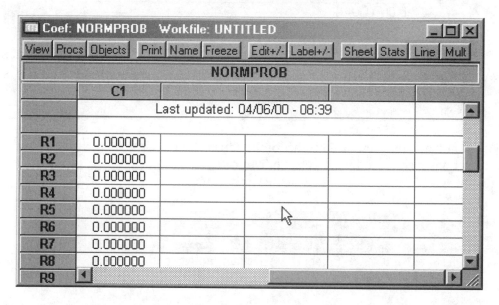

- Alternatively, on the EViews command line type **coef(10) normprob** and **enter**

- On the command line, type the following series of commands

      normprob(1) = (6-3)/3
      normprob(2) = (4-3)/3
      normprob(3) = @cnorm(normprob(1))-@cnorm(normprob(2))

As you type in the commands, you will see in the cells of **normprob** the values as they are computed

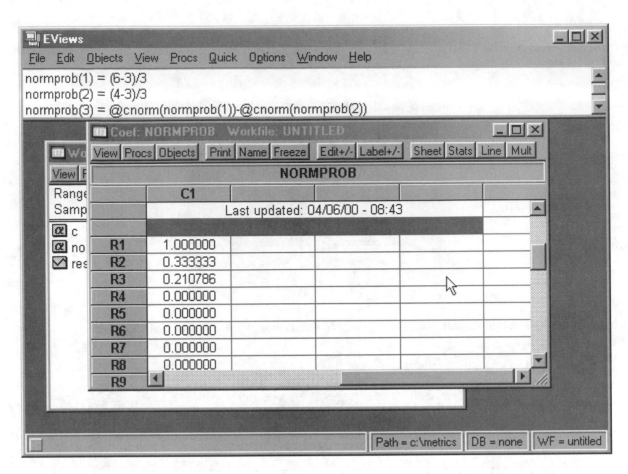

- Click on the **x** in the upper right hand corner of the spreadsheet to close it. You will note that the workfile, as yet unsaved, includes the vector **normprob**.
- To save the file, click on the **save** button on the workfile toolbar

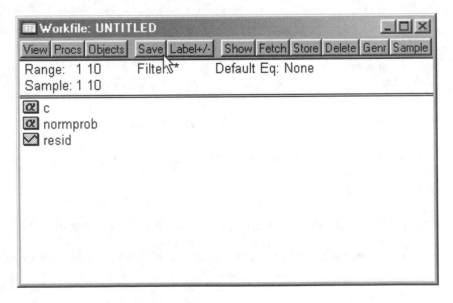

- Name the workfile *ch-2*, or something similar

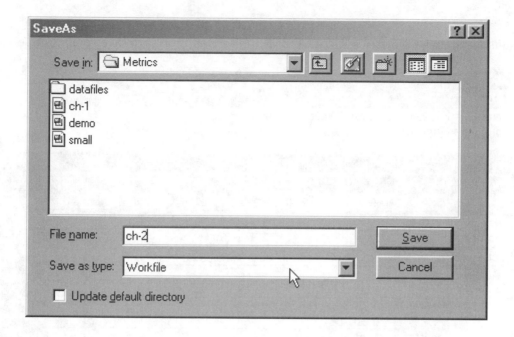

2.2   *Computing Normal Distribution Percentiles*

The function **@qnorm(p)** returns the percentile value **z** from a standard normal probability density, such that **P(Z<z) = p**. For example, probability of .10 falls to the **left** of −1.28.

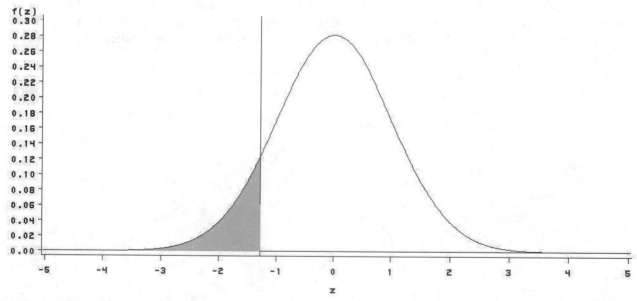

- Double click on **normprob** in the workfile to re-open the spreadsheet view. On the command line, type

```
normprob(4) = @qnorm(.10)
```

• The results are shown in rows R1-R4 in NORMPROB. <u>Don't forget to save your workfile</u>.

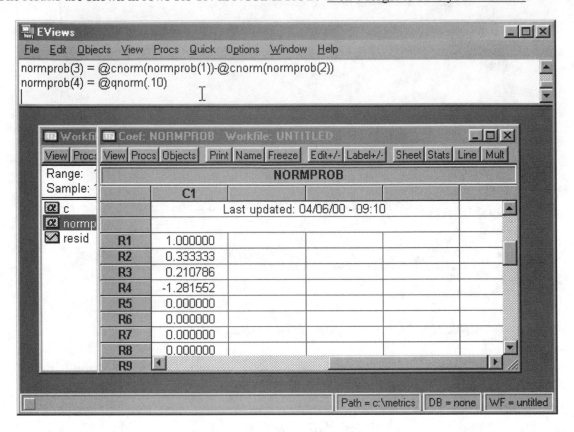

EViews will compute similar probabilities for many types of random variables. Click on **Help/Function Reference**. Scroll down to the section entitled *Statistical Distribution Functions*. There you will find a long list of probability distributions for which EViews can compute cumulative probabilities and percentiles. You have heard of some, like the **Binomial**. Many others will not be familiar. We will use several of these distributions in later chapters, such as the **Chi-square**, the **F-distribution** and **Student's *t*-distribution**.

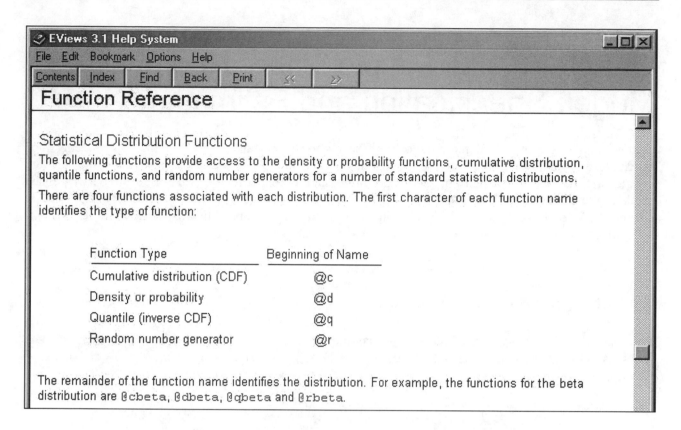

Function Reference

Statistical Distribution Functions

The following functions provide access to the density or probability functions, cumulative distribution, quantile functions, and random number generators for a number of standard statistical distributions.

There are four functions associated with each distribution. The first character of each function name identifies the type of function:

Function Type	Beginning of Name
Cumulative distribution (CDF)	@c
Density or probability	@d
Quantile (inverse CDF)	@q
Random number generator	@r

The remainder of the function name identifies the distribution. For example, the functions for the beta distribution are @cbeta, @dbeta, @qbeta and @rbeta.

Chapter 3 The Simple Linear Regression Model: Specification and Estimation

In this chapter we introduce the simple linear regression model and estimate a model of weekly food expenditure. We also demonstrate the plotting capabilities of EViews and show how to use the software to calculate the income elasticity of food expenditure, and to predict food expenditure from our regression results. We open the workfile *table3-1.wf1*, where we find the series y_t (food expenditure) and x_t (weekly income). We note that the workfile also includes containers for the estimated coefficients C, and the residuals RESID, of the most recent regression model we estimate:

3.1 Plotting the Food Expenditure Data

To create the scatter diagram of the food expenditure data found in Figure 3.6 of *UE/2*, click on the x series to select it. Next, while holding the **<ctrl>** button down, click on the y series to add it to the selection.

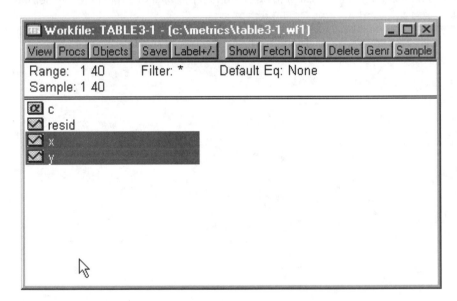

Important Note: The order in which we select variables in the EViews workfile matters. The variable selected first will be plotted on the x-axis.

- Next, double-click anywhere on the highlighted series and select Open Group to view the series.

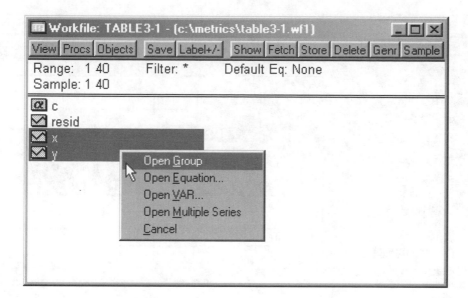

This opens the spreadsheet view of the data.

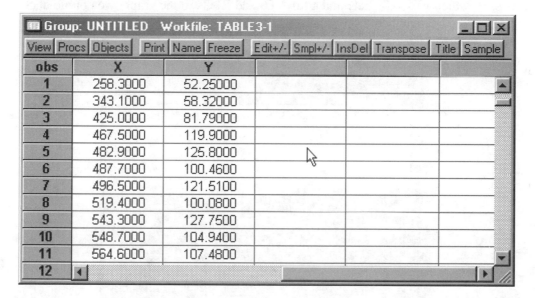

- We change the group's view by clicking on **View**.
- To plot a scatter diagram select **Graph/Scatter/Simple Scatter** as shown below:

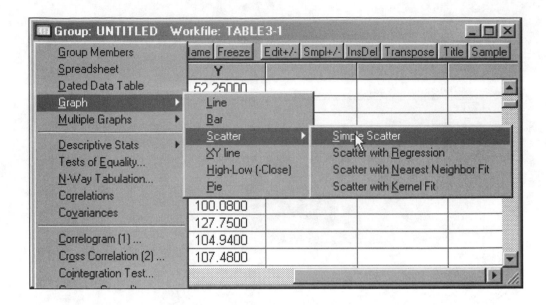

A plot appears, to which we add labels and a title. To add labels to the graph, we double-click on the axes labels "x" and "y" and change them accordingly.

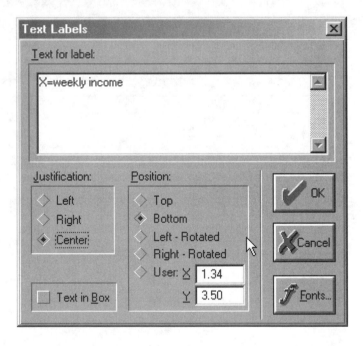

- To add the graph title, we right-click anywhere on the graph and select **Add text**.

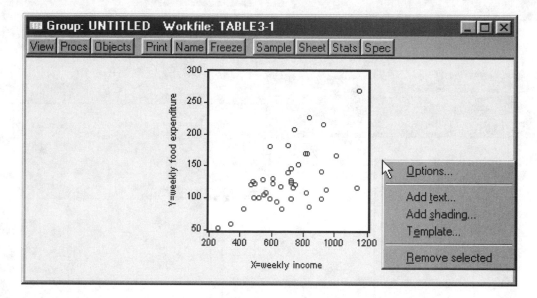

- After entering the title in the **Text for label** field, we select **Center** for the title's justification and **Top** for its position.

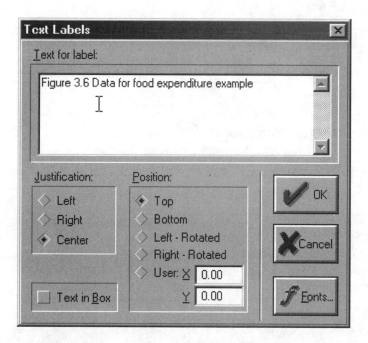

The plot appears with labels and a title.

- To save this figure, click on **Name**, type in *Figure3_6* and click **OK**.

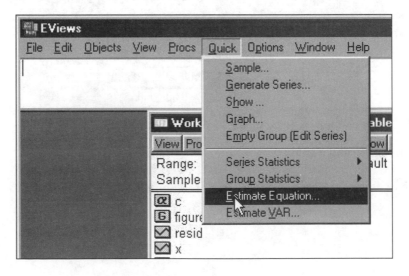

3.2 Estimating a Simple Regression

To estimate the parameters b_1 and b_2 of the food expenditure equation, we select **Quick/Estimate Equation** from the EViews menubar.

In the Equation Specification dialog box, type the dependent variable **y** first, **c** (which is EViews notation for the intercept term, or constant), and then the independent variable **x**. Note in the **Estimation Settings** window, the **Method** is **Least Squares** and the **Sample** is **1 40**. Click **OK**.

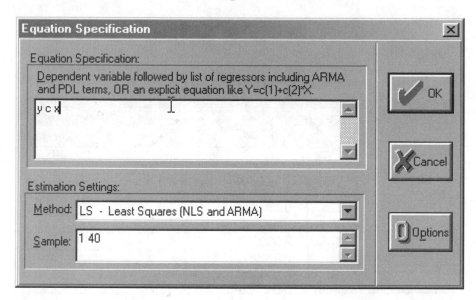

The estimated regression output appears. EViews produces an equation object in its default **Stats** view. We can name the equation object to save it permanently in our workfile by clicking on **Name** in the equation's toolbar. We have used the text's equation number and named this equation **EQ3_3_9**.

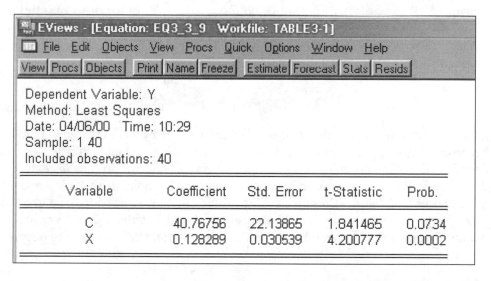

Note the estimated coefficient b_1, the intercept in our food expenditure model is recorded as the coefficient on the variable C in EViews. C is the EViews term for the constant in a regression model. Note that we cannot name any of our variables C since this term is reserved exclusively for the constant or "intercept" in a regression model. Our EViews output shows $b_1 = 40.7676$. The estimated value of the slope coefficient on the variable weekly income (X) is $b_2 = 0.1283$, as recorded in *UE/2*. The interpretation of b_2 is: for every \$1 increase in weekly income we estimate that there is about a 13 cent increase in weekly food expenditure, holding all other factors constant.

In the workfile window, double click on the vector **c**. It always contains the estimated coefficients from the most recent regression. The vector **resid** always contains the least squares residuals from the most recent regression.

To calculate the income elasticity of demand reported in equation (3.3.14) of the text, in the EViews command window type the following command and press the **<Enter>** key:

scalar elast = eq3_3_9.@coefs(2)*@mean(x)/@mean(y)   **income elasticity**

Note that the scalar **elast** is a single number. To view this number, double-click on **elast** in the workfile and its value appears in the status line at the bottom of the EViews main window.

This command works by referring to the least squares estimate b_2 by the name **eq3_3_9.@coefs(2).** We can do this because EViews saves estimated coefficients from each equation in a vector called **@coefs**. To refer to a coefficients of a particular regression, such as eq3_3_9, we precede **@coefs** by the name of the equation and a period, as we have done in **eq3_3_9.@coefs(2)**, indicating which element of the vector we want in parentheses. EViews saves many other values after a regression. To see these, click on **Help/Index**, then type in **Regression**, select **Regression,saved results**. For more on these naming conventions within EViews go back to the **Index**, and see **Regression statistics,how to access**.

3.3 Plotting a Simple Regression

To create a graph of the regression line:
  • On the main window toolbar, click on **Quick/Graph**.

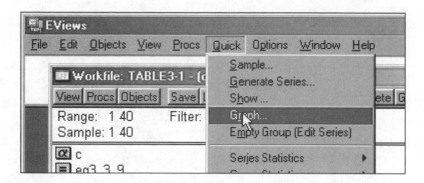

- In the **Series list** box that appears, type **x y**. Click **OK**.
- Under **Graph Type**, select **Scatter Diagram**.

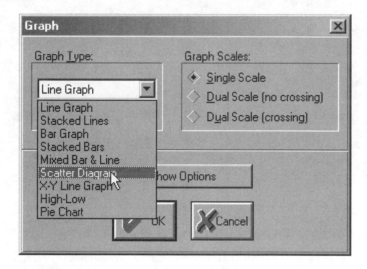

- Click **Show Options**.
- In the lower right hand area of the dialog box that opens, Under **Scatter Diagram:**, select **Regression line**. Click **OK**.

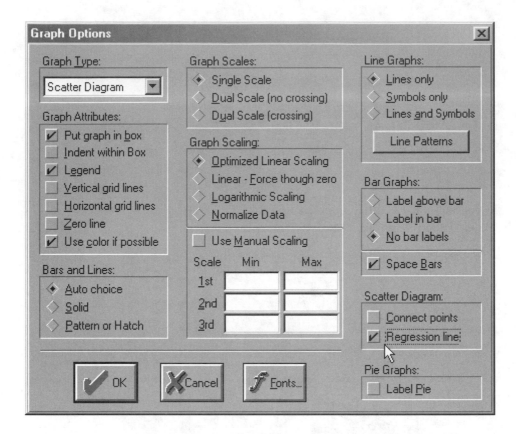

The plot of the fitted regression appears, like Figure 3.9 in your text. Once again you can add labels and a title. The figure can be pasted into a document by following the steps in Chapter 1.6 of this handbook.

3.4 Plotting the Least Squares Residuals

To create a graph of the residuals against income:

- In the workfile window, click on **Quick/Graph**.
- In the **Series list** box that appears, type **income resid**. Click **OK**.
- Under **Graph Type**, select **Scatter Diagram**. Click **OK**.

To examine the residuals and fitted values, in the window containing the regression results, click **View/Actual, Fitted Residual/ Actual, Fitted Residual Table**

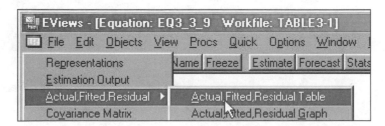

This view shows a table containing the y values, the fitted values $\hat{y}$ and the least squares residuals $\hat{e}$.

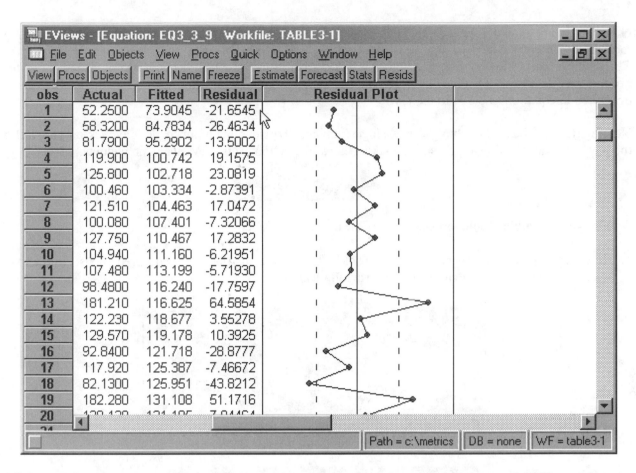

Click on **View/Representations**. There you see the estimated equation in several different formats. Select the text of the equation listed under **Substituted Coefficients**. We can choose **Edit/Copy** from the EViews menubar, or we can simply use the keyboard shortcut **Ctrl+C** to copy the equation representation to the clipboard. Finally, we can paste the equation into a word processing document using **Edit/Paste** from the word processor's menubar, or by using the keyboard shortcut **Ctrl+V**. The result is:

$$Y = 40.76755647 + 0.1282886011*X$$

which we then edit to appear as it does in equation (3.3.10) the text

$$y_t = 40.7676 + 0.1283x_t.$$

- Click on **View/Estimation Output**. This returns you to the regression results.

3.5 Using EViews to Predict with a Simple Regression Model

To predict weekly food expenditure for a household with a weekly income of $750, type the following command in the EViews command window and press the **<Enter>** key:

scalar yhat750 = 40.7676 + 0.1283*(750)   **predicted value of y when x = 750**

Note: A quick way to retrieve the equation is to click on **View/Representations** from the eq3_3_9 toolbar and copy the text of the equation as listed under **Substituted Coefficients** onto the clipboard. Then simply paste the equation text into the EViews command window. This is one of EViews' greatest productivity features. Of course, some editing is necessary to match the rounding of the coefficients as presented in equation (3.3.15) in the text.

Note again that the scalar **yhat750** is a single number. To view this number, double-click on **yhat750** in the workfile and its value appears in the status line at the bottom of the EViews main window.

A more general, and flexible, procedure uses the power of EViews

1. In order to predict we must enter additional x observations at which we want predictions. In the main workfile window, click **Procs/Change workfile Range**.

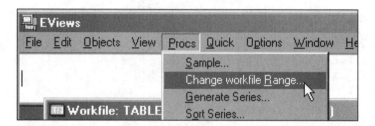

2. Change the **End** observation to 43.

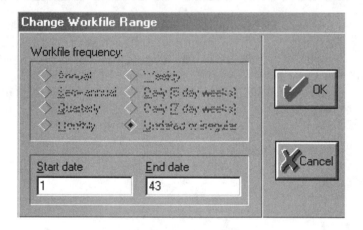

3. Next we must edit the x (income) series to enter the new data. Double click on the variable name **x** in the main window, and click the **Edit+/-** button in the series window, which puts EViews in **edit mode**.

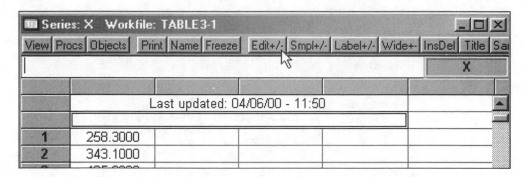

4. Scroll to the bottom and you see **NA** in the cells for observations 41-43. Click the cell for observation 41 and enter 750. Enter 800 and 850 in cells 42 and 43, respectively. When you are done, click the **Edit+/-** button again to turn off the edit mode.

5. To forecast, first re-estimate the model with the original data. Click on **Quick/Estimate Equation**. Enter the equation. Note that the observations used are 1-40.

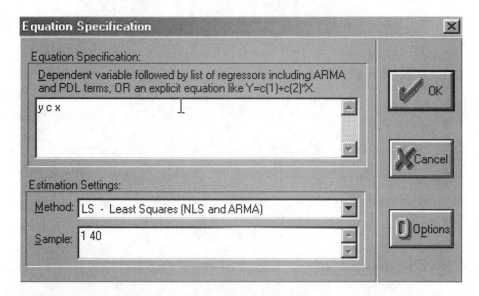

6. To forecast with the estimated model, click on the **Forecast** button in the equation window.

7. The following dialog box appears:

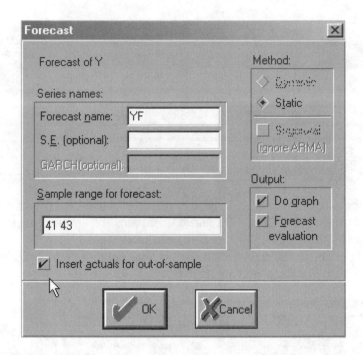

EViews automatically assigns the name **YF** to the forecast series, so if you want a different name enter it. Specify the **Sample range for forecast** to be 41 to 43. For now, ignore the other options. Click **OK**.

8. A graph appears showing the fitted line for observations 41-43 along with lines labeled ±2 S.E. We will discuss these in Chapter 5. To see the fitted values themselves, in the workfile window, double click on the series named **YF** and scroll to the bottom. There you see the three forecast values corresponding to incomes 750, 800 and 850. The value in cell 41,

$$136.984007255$$

is the predicted value shown in Chapter 3.3.3b.

Chapter 4 Properties of the Least Squares Estimators

This chapter examines some important properties of the least squares estimators. Accordingly, we demonstrate the storage and retrieval in EViews of the regression statistics that correspond to these properties.

4.1 The Estimated Variances and Covariances for the Food Expenditure Example

Once again we open the workfile *table3-1.wf1*, where we find the EViews equation object EQ3_3_9. If you did not save it, then
- On the main menu bar click **Quick/Estimate Equation**.
- In the dialog box type **y c x**. Click **OK**.
- Click on **Name**. Type in EQ3_3_9.

```
Equation: EQ3_3_9  Workfile: TABLE3-1                    _ □ ×
View Procs Objects  Print Name Freeze  Estimate Forecast Stats Resids

Dependent Variable: Y
Method: Least Squares
Date: 04/10/00   Time: 12:28
Sample: 1 40
Included observations: 40
```

Variable	Coefficient	Std. Error	t-Statistic	Prob.
C	40.76756	22.13865	1.841465	0.0734
X	0.128289	0.030539	4.200777	0.0002

R-squared	0.317118	Mean dependent var	130.3130
Adjusted R-squared	0.299148	S.D. dependent var	45.15857
S.E. of regression	37.80536	Akaike info criterion	10.15149
Sum squared resid	54311.33	Schwarz criterion	10.23593
Log likelihood	-201.0297	F-statistic	17.64653
Durbin-Watson stat	2.370373	Prob(F-statistic)	0.000155

Some items of interest in the output are:

- The sum of squared least squares residuals, $\sum \hat{e}_t^2$, appears in the output as "**Sum squared resid** 54311.33"
- EViews does not explicitly show the degrees of freedom, $T-2$, but it does provide the number of observations, **Included observations**: 40.

- The estimated value of the error variance is $\hat{\sigma}^2 = \sum \hat{e}_t^2/(T-2)$. EViews reports the value of the estimated standard deviation $\hat{\sigma}$ as "**S.E. of regression** 37.80536," which stands for "Standard Error of the Regression." Do not confuse this with "**S.D. dependent var** 45.15857" which is the sample standard deviation of the y values.
- To view the estimated variances and covariances of the least squares estimators, in the estimation output window, click View, Covariance Matrix.

Equation: EQ3_3_9 Workfile: TABLE3-1			
View	Procs	Objects	Print	Name	Freeze	Estimate	Forecast	Stats
Coefficient Covariance Matrix			
	C	**X**		
C	490.1200	-0.650987		
X	-0.650987	0.000933		

- The estimated standard errors of the coefficients se(b_1) = 22.14 and se(b_2) = 0.03 are presented in the third column under the heading **Std. Error**. The estimated variances of the coefficients, var(b_1) = 490.12 and var(b_2) = 0.0009326 as reported in the text, are simply the squares of their respective standard errors, ie, var(b_1) = [se(b_1)]^2, and var(b_2) = [se(b_2)]^2.

4.2   Storing Results

To create a permanent storage location in the workfile for the equation (3.3.9) output, enter the following commands in the EViews command window, each followed by pressing the <Enter> key:

coef(6) cova	**Creates a storage vector**
cova(1) = eq3_3_9.@se^2	**error variance (σ^2)**
cova(2) = eq3_3_9.@stderrs(1)^2	**variance of b_1 [var(b_1)]**
cova(3) = eq3_3_9.@stderrs(1)	**standard error of b_1 [se(b_1)]**
cova(4) = eq3_3_9.@stderrs(2)^2	**variance of b_2 [var(b_2)]**
cova(5) = eq3_3_9.@stderrs(2)	**standard error of b_2 [se(b_2)]**
cova(6) = eq3_3_9.@cov(1,2)	**covariance of b_1,b_2 [cov(b_1,b_2)]**

The result of this series of commands is the storage vector **cova**, as shown on the next page.

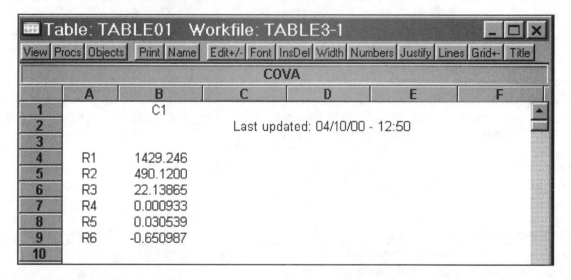

EViews allows us to create an editable table from this storage vector. To do so, simply click on **Freeze** from the storage vector **cova**'s toolbar, and name the resulting table **TABLE01**.

The new table of results has toolbar buttons that allow for a variety of formatting options, including Grid+-, Justify, Lines, Title, and Font. We created **TABLE01** below by adding gridlines, and editing cells A5 to A10 to include labels for the variance and standard error estimates. Play with the editing tools in the **FREEZE** mode to see their capabilities.

	A	B	C	D	E	F
Table: TABLE01 Workfile: TABLE3-1						
View Procs Objects Print Name Edit+/- Font InsDel Width Numbers Justify Lines Grid+- Title						
1		Estimate				
2	var(e)	1429.246				
3	var(b1)	490.1200				
4	se(b1)	22.13865				
5	var(b2)	0.000933				
6	se(b2)	0.030539				
7	cov(b1,b2)	-0.650987				
8						

4.3   Working with Regression Statistics

Every time a regression is run in EViews a number of statistics, such as those above, are stored in memory for later use. If you click on EViews **Help** and examine the documentation for ordinary least squares regression you will see the entire list, but for now we focus on a few that are relevant for Chapter 4.

The regression statistics reported in the estimation output view are stored with the equation and are accessible through special @-functions. You can retrieve any of these statistics for further analysis by using these functions in genr, scalar, or matrix expressions. If a particular statistic is not computed for a given estimation method, the function will return an NA.

There are two kinds of @-functions: those that return a scalar value, and those that return matrices or vectors. Those that return scalar values can be saved into a storage vector as we did in the previous section.

Functions that return scalar values:

@se	standard error of the regression
@ssr	sum of squared residuals
@regobs	number of observations in regression
@meandep	mean of the dependent variable
@sddep	standard deviation of the dependent variable
@ncoef	total number of estimated coefficients
@coefs(i)	coefficient i, where i is given by the order in which the coefficients appear in the representations view
@stderrs(i)	standard error for coefficient i
@coefcov(i,j)	covariance of coefficients i and j

Functions that return vector or matrix objects:

@coefs	vector of coefficient values
@stderrs	vector of standard errors for the coefficients
@cov	matrix containing the coefficient covariance matrix

To save matrices, we proceed as follows. In the command window, type

> matrix covb=eq3_3_9.@coefcov.

This creates a "matrix object" called **covb** which contains the estimated variances and covariances of the least squares estimators. In the workfile window, double click on the matrix **covb** to view the matrix.

4.4   *Plots of Least Squares Residuals*

After estimating a regression model, researchers often want to investigate the pattern of the least squares residuals (e_t). In subsequent chapters, we will discuss at length the many techniques that EViews offers for analyzing least squares residuals. For now we restrict our attention to the simple tabular presentation of the residuals as found in Table 4.1 in the text. From the EQ3_3_9 object's toolbar, select **View/Actual,Fitted,Residual/Actual,Fitted,Residual Table**.

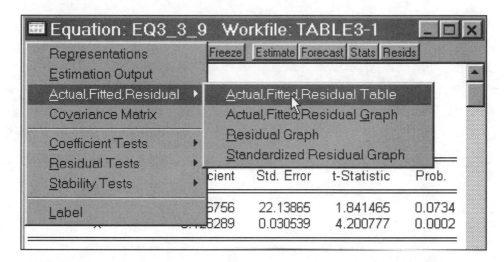

The result is the following table and residual plot, of which we display the first eleven observations matching Table 4.1 in the text.

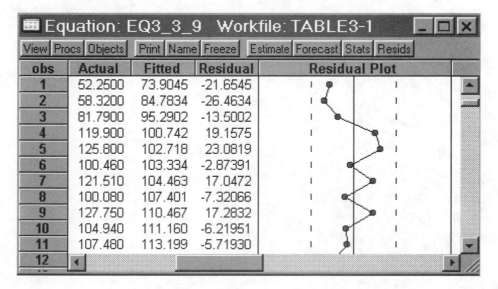

In the chapters ahead, we will find many occasions to consult the residual table and plot pictured here as well as its associated graph. For now, note that the solid line down the middle of the plot is the "zero" line; a dot centered over this line indicates visually that the actual and fitted data points coincide so that the residual (e_t) equals zero. Dots lying to the right of the zero line indicate positive residuals and dots lying to the left of the zero line indicate negative residuals.

Chapter 5 Inference in the Simple Regression Model

While estimation is a critical first step in the practice of econometrics, most researchers intend to use their models to draw inferences and make predictions about economic behavior. In this chapter we learn how to implement interval estimation, hypothesis testing, and prediction procedures using EViews. Once again we open the workfile *table3-1.wf1*, where we find the EViews equation object EQ3_3_9.

5.1   Interval Estimation Using the Food Expenditure Data

To construct interval estimates we will use EViews' stored regression results, as demonstrated in Chapter 4.2.3. We will also make use of EViews built in statistical functions. For each distribution (see **Function reference** in EViews Help) four statistical functions are provided. The two we will make use of are the **cumulative distribution** (CDF) and the **quantile** (Inverse CDF) functions.

- The CDF is given by the function **@ctdist(x,v)**. This function returns the **probability** that a t-random variable with **v** degrees of freedom falls to the left of **x**. That is,

$$@ctdist(x,v) = P\left[\, t_{(v)} \le x \,\right].$$

- The quantile function **@qtdist(p,v)** computes the **critical value** of a t-random variable with **v** degrees of freedom such that probability **p** falls to the left of it. For example, if we specify *tcrit=@qtdist(.975,38)*, then

$$P\left[\, t_{(38)} \le tcrit \,\right] = .975 .$$

To generate the 95% confidence interval $[b_2 - t_c se(b_2),\ b_2 + t_c se(b_2)]$ presented in equation (5.1.13), enter the following commands in the EViews command window, pressing the **<Enter>** key after each:

```
coef(2) confint
confint(1) = eq3_3_9.@coefs(2) - @qtdist(.975,38)*eq3_3_9.@stderrs(2)
confint(2) = eq3_3_9.@coefs(2) + @qtdist(.975,38)*eq3_3_9.@stderrs(2)
```

where   eq3_3_9.@coefs(2) = b_2
             eq3_3_9.@stderrs(2) = $se(b_2)$
             @qtdist(.975,38) = t_c

The preceding commands produce the coefficient vector **confint** as shown below

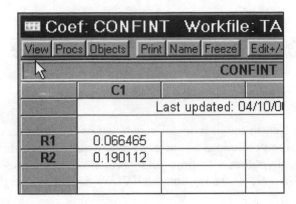

We can create a more presentable table by choosing **Freeze** from **confint's** toolbar and naming the resulting table **TABLE02**, which we can then edit to include a title, gridlines, and labels as shown in Chapter 4.2 of this book. Alternatively, highlight the data cells and copy them, by clicking **Edit/Copy**, or use the key stroke **Ctrl+C**.

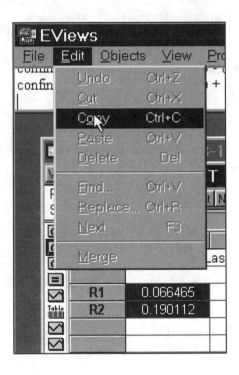

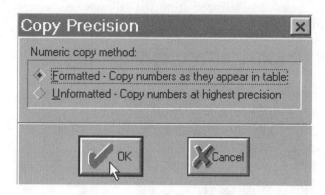

You will be presented with a dialog box asking whether the data are to be formatted as on the screen or not. Click **Formatted** and **OK**. The cells are copied to the Windows clipboard. If you open a Microsoft Word document you can **paste** the cells into the document as a table, which will look like this

0.066465

0.190112

Then you can edit the table to add grid-lines, change the font, add labels and a title.

Interval Estimates for B2	
lower	0.066465
upper	0.190112

These values differ slightly from those in Result (R5.2) in the text due to rounding. The textbook's computations are carried out using the rounded values shown there. EViews' computations are carried out with more significant digits.

5.2   A Two-Tailed Hypothesis Test

In this section we test the hypothesis that weekly food expenditures rise by \$10 when weekly income rises by \$100. Such a hypothesis can be stated as $\beta_2 = 0.1$. To conduct this test, in the EViews command window type the following commands (do not type the comments in the bold font), each followed by the **<Enter>** key:

```
coef(10) ttest                  storage vector
ttest(1)=eq3_3_9.@coefs(2)      b₂
ttest(2)=eq3_3_9.@stderrs(2)    se(b₂)
ttest(3)=(ttest(1)-.10)/ttest(2)   t-statistic
ttest(4)=@abs(ttest(3))         |t-statistic|
ttest(5)=1-@ctdist(ttest(4),38)   P[t(38)≥ |t-statistic|]
ttest(6)=2*ttest(5)             two-tailed p-value
```

This is a two-tailed test that places half of the rejection region in each tail of the t-distribution. The p-value is the sum of the computed areas to the right of the t-statistic in the upper tail and to the left of the t-statistic in the lower tail. Double-click on the coefficient vector **ttest** in your workfile to see the results of this test. Compare your results to those in Chapter 5.2.5 of *UE/2*.

The results of the *t*-test in a table object frozen from the storage vector **ttest**, named **TABLE03**, and edited to include a title, gridlines, numeric formatting, and labels are:

	A	B	C
		statistic	
1		statistic	
2	b2	0.128289	
3	se(b2)	0.030539	
4	t-stat	0.926303	
5	abs(t-stat)	0.926303	
6	p/2	0.180067	
7	p	0.360135	

Test of the Hypothesis B2 = 0.1

Copying the table results, pasting them into a document and editing the resulting table yields

ttest	
b_2	0.128289
$se(b_2)$	0.030539
t-stat	0.926303
abs(t-stat)	0.926303
p/2	0.180067
p	0.360135

5.3   A Significance Test in the Food Expenditure Model

Here we demonstrate a test of the statistical significance of the slope coefficient β_2 from the food expenditure model. This tests the null hypothesis: H_0: $\beta_2 = 0$ against the alternative hypothesis H_1: $\beta_2 \neq 0$. This topic is discussed in Chapter 5.1.8 of *UE/2*. In words, the significance test answers the question: "Does the independent variable weekly income have any effect at all on weekly food expenditures?" To conduct this test in EViews, we proceed as we did above, the only difference being that our hypothesized value of β_2 under the null hypothesis is now zero instead of 0.1. Enter the following commands in the EViews command window:

```
coef(3) sigtest                                    Creates a storage vector
sigtest(1) = eq3_3_9.@coefs(2)/eq3_3_9.@stderrs(2)  t-statistic
sigtest(2) = @qtdist(.975,38)                       critical value tc
sigtest(3) = 2*(1-@ctdist(sigtest(1),38))           p-value
```

Like the more general hypothesis test we conducted above, the significance test is a two-tailed test that places half of the rejection region in each tail of the *t*-distribution. The *p*-value is the sum of the computed areas to the right of the *t*-statistic in the upper tail and to the left of the *t*-statistic in the lower tail. Double-click on the coefficient vector **sigtest** in your workfile to see the results of this test.

The EViews output for any regression equation contains all the information relevant to the significance test except the critical value t_c. For equation (3.3.9) the statistical output is:

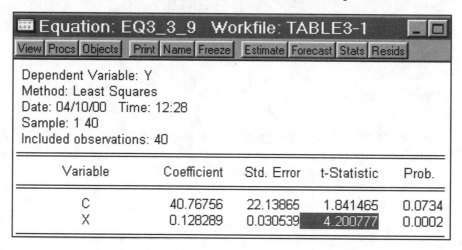

Highlighted in the fourth column labeled "t-Statistic", to the right of the variable X, we find the t-statistic that we calculated above, 4.200. To the right of the t-statistic is the p-value, 0.000155, that we calculated above, here rounded to 0.0002. The only test component included in our procedure above yet missing from the statistical output for equation (3.3.9) is the critical value t_c. In practice, researchers usually examine the p-value and compare it to the chosen level of significance, α. The rejection rule is: "If the p-value of a hypothesis test is smaller than the chosen level of significance, α, reject the null hypothesis." Throughout the text, unless otherwise stated, we choose a significance level $\alpha = .05$. Comparing the p-value, .0002, for the t-statistic calculated under the null hypothesis $H_0: \beta_2 = 0$ to our significance level $\alpha = .05$, we find that the p-value is less than the significance level, hence we reject $H_0: \beta_2 = 0$ in favor of H_1: $\beta_2 \neq 0$. Our decision means that the independent variable weekly income has a statistically significant effect on weekly food expenditures.   For the null hypothesis $H_0: \beta_1 = 0$, we find that the p-value, .0734 exceeds our significance level, $\alpha = .05$, hence we fail to reject $H_0: \beta_1 = 0$.

5.4   One-Tailed Tests in the Food Expenditure Model

In this section we demonstrate how to carry out some one-tailed tests. Pay particular attention to the computation of p-values and critical values.

5.4.1 Alternative Greater Than (>)

Suppose that we wish to test the hypothesis that $\beta_2 = .10$ against the alternative $\beta_2 > .10$ at the $\alpha = .05$ level of significance. The computation of the t-statistic is identical to the computation in the two-tailed test. The critical value and p-value are only in the right-tail of the t-density.

In the EViews command window, enter the following commands.

```
coef(3) ttest1                              storage vector
ttest1(1)=(eq3_3_9.@coefs(2)-.10)/eq3_3_9.@stderrs(2)  t-stat
ttest1(2)=@qtdist(.95,38)                   right tail critical value
ttest1(3)=1-@ctdist(ttest1(1),38)           p-value in right tail
```

In this one-tailed test the critical value has the probability of a type I error, $\alpha = .05$, in the right-tail only. The p-value also is computed as the area to the right of the computed t-statistic value. The outcome is

ttest1	
t-stat	0.926303
t-crit	1.685954
p	0.180067

5.4.2 Alternative Less Than (<)

Suppose that we wish to test the hypothesis that $\beta_2 = .10$ against the alternative $\beta_2 < .10$ at the $\alpha = .05$ level of significance. The computation of the t-statistic is identical to the computation in the two-tailed test. The critical value and p-value are only in the left-tail of the t-density.

In the EViews command window, enter the following commands.

```
coef(2) ttest2                        storage vector
ttest2(1)=@qtdist(.05,38)             left tail critical value
ttest2(2)=@ctdist(ttest1(1),38)       p-value in left tail
```

Note in the last line that we use an element of the vector **ttest1**. The result is

ttest2	
t-stat	-1.685954
p	0.819933

5.4.3 One-Tailed Test of Significance

Economic theory suggests that weekly food expenditures should increase with weekly income. Theory implies the null hypothesis H_0: $\beta_2 = 0$ and the alternative hypothesis H_1: $\beta_2 > 0$. The appropriate hypothesis test is one-tailed. To conduct this test in EViews, enter the following commands in the EViews command window:

```
coef(3) sig1test                                  Creates a storage vector
sig1test(1) = eq3_3_9.@coefs(2)/eq3_3_9.@stderrs(2)   t-statistic
sig1test(2) = @qtdist(.95,38)                     critical value t_c
sig1test(3) = 1-@ctdist(sig1test(1),38)           p-value
```

Note two differences in implementing the one-tailed test. First, we no longer split the rejection region into the two tails of the distribution. Our rejection region now lies entirely to the right of the critical value, t_c, and is comprised of α rather than $\alpha/2$ as in the two-tailed test. Hence we use $1 - \alpha = .95$ rather than $1 - \alpha/2 = 0.975$ as the first parameter in the @qdist($\cdot$) function to calculate the critical value t_c. Second, our formula for the p-value reflects the one-tailed rejection region in that we no longer multiply the formula 1 - @ctdist($\cdot$) by two. This test produces the coefficient storage vector **sig1test**, which we freeze as **table04**.

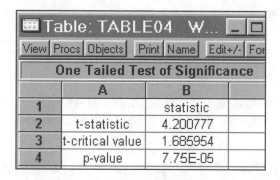

Since our test statistic, 4.201, exceeds the t-critical value 1.686, we reject H_0: $\beta_2 = 0$ in favor of the alternative hypothesis H_1: $\beta_2 > 0$. We make the same decision under our alternative rejection rule, namely, since the p-value, 0.0000775, is less than our chosen significance level $\alpha = .05$, we reject the null hypothesis that $\beta_2 = 0$.

5.5   Prediction in the Food Expenditure Model

5.5.1   Constructing the Interval

To create a prediction interval for our point prediction from the food expenditure model we need first to estimate the standard error of the forecast. Enter the following commands in the EViews command window:

coef(8) predint	**Creates a storage vector**
predint(1) = @qtdist(.975,38)	**critical value (t_c)**
predint(2) = eq3_3_9.@se^2	**error varance (σ^2)**
predint(3) = 1 + 1/eq3_3_9.@regobs	**[1 + 1/T]**
predint(4) = (750 - @mean(x))^2	**[x_0 – mean(x)] squared**
predint(5) = @var(x)*(eq3_3_9.@regobs - 1)	**variations in x**
predint(6) = (predint(2)*(predint(3)+predint(4)/predint(5)))^.5	**forecast std. error [se(f)]**
predint(7) = 136.98 - predint(1)*predint(6)	**Lower bound**
predint(8) = 136.98 + predint(1)*predint(6)	**Upper bound**

These commands produce the storage vector **predint**, which we freeze and edit to produce the following table:

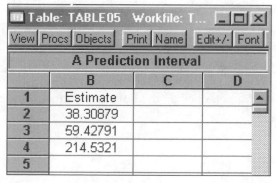

5.5.2 Predicting Using EViews

The "brute force" method used above clearly works, but EViews makes this task much easier, as the following steps illustrate.

- In order to predict we must enter additional x observations at which we want predictions. In the main workfile window, click **Procs/Change workfile Range**. Change the End observation to 43 and click **OK**.

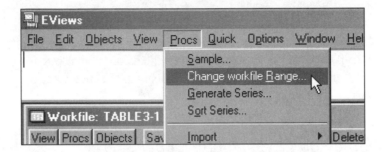

- Next we must edit the x (income) series to enter the new data. Double click on the variable name income in the main window, and click the **Edit+/-** button in the series window, which puts EViews in edit mode. Scroll to the bottom and you see NA in the cells for observations 41-43. Click the cell for observation 41 and enter 750. Enter 800 and 850 in cells 42 and 43, respectively. When you are done, click the **Edit+/-** button again to turn off the edit mode.
- To forecast, first re-estimate the model with the original data, observations 1-40.

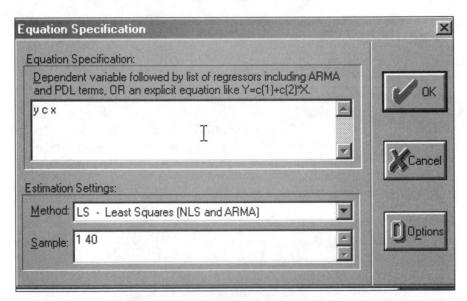

- To forecast with the estimated model, click on the **Forecast** button in the equation window.

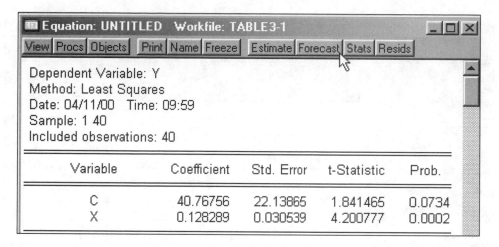

- The following dialog box appears:

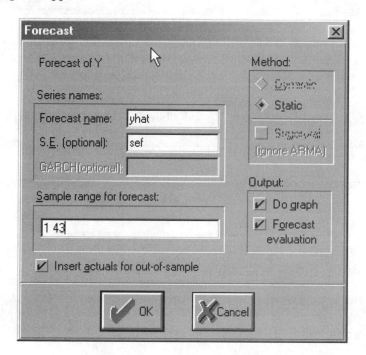

EViews automatically assigns the name **YF** to the forecast series, so if you want a different name enter it, say **yhat**. Enter a name for "S.E.", which is the standard error of the forecast, **sef**. Specify the **Sample range for forecast** to be 1 to 43. For now, ignore the other options. Click **OK**.

- A graph appears showing the fitted line for observations 1-43 along with lines labeled ±2 S.E. This graph shows the fitted values and approximate 95% prediction interval. To see the fitted values themselves, in the workfile window, double click on the series named **yhat** and scroll to the bottom. There you see the three forecast values corresponding to incomes 750, 800 and 850. The value in cell 41 is the value given in *UE/2* for predicted food expenditure when income is $750.

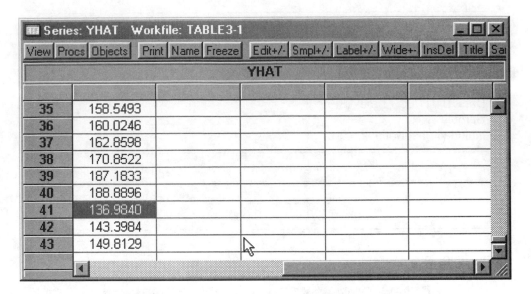

- To plot an actual 95% prediction interval we first must create the upper and lower bounds. First we must change the sample with which we are working. On the workfile tool bar select the **sample button**.

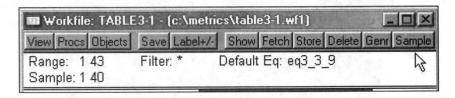

- Enter **1 43**. In the command window type

      genr yhatu = yhat + @qtdist(.975,38)*sef
      genr yhatl = yhat - @qtdist(.975,38)*sef

- Click on **Quick/Graph**, which opens the following dialog window. Enter **x**, which is income (the first variable listed will go on the horizontal axis, all other variables will be plotted against it on the vertical axis), **yhat yhatl yhatu**. Click **OK.**

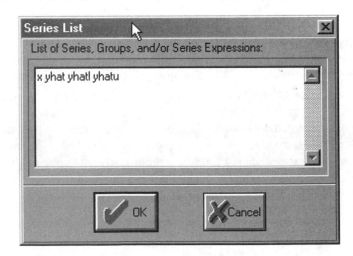

- Select **X-Y line graph**, click **OK**. Name it **yhat_l_u**.

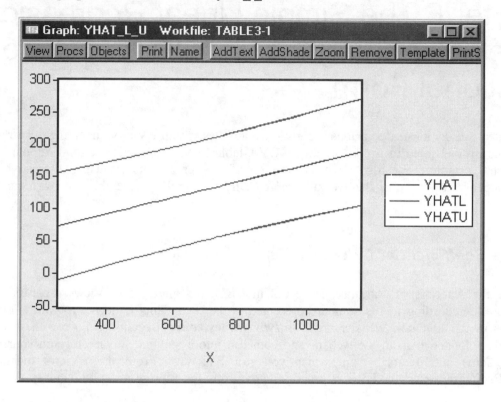

- Inspect the series **x yhat yhatl yhatu** to verify that at income $750 the prediction interval is the same as the one in the text.

Chapter 6 The Simple Linear Regression Model: Reporting the Results and Choosing Functional Form

In this chapter, we demonstrate various reporting capabilities within EViews, including our first use of an EViews program dedicated to producing an ANOVA table for decomposing the total sample variation of the dependent variable. We also show how to specify regression models using alternative functional forms. Once again we open the workfile *table3-1.wf1*, where we find the EViews equation object EQ3_3_9.

6.1   The Coefficient of Determination

To generate the Analysis of Variance Table 6.2 in *UE/2*, we employ an EViews program designed to format the table according to the standard presented in the text. This EViews program is available for download from the textbook website at: **http://www.wiley.com/college/hill**. To use the program, you must have downloaded it from the website and copied it into a suitable subdirectory on your hard drive, ideally the same subdirectory from which you run EViews. From the EViews menubar, select **File/Open/Program**. Select the EViews program **anova** from the appropriate subdirectory.

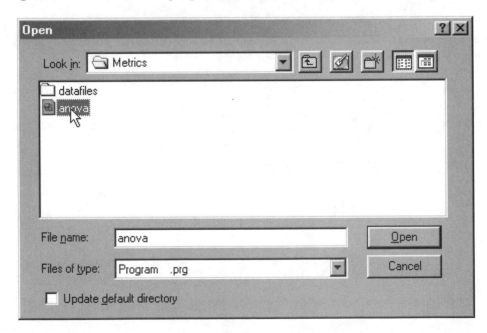

The program **anova** opens in the EViews main window.

Note: We can use this program to produce an analysis of variance table for the most recent regression in any workfile. All we need to do is make sure the filename listed after the workfile statement is the appropriate one, in this case, *table3-1*.

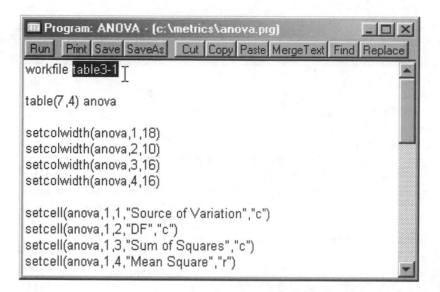

- To run the program, click **Run** from the program's toolbar, and then click **OK**.

The analysis of variance table, Table 6.2 in *UE/2*, opens in the EViews main window. We added a title by pressing the **Title** button on the table object's toolbar and entering our desired title.

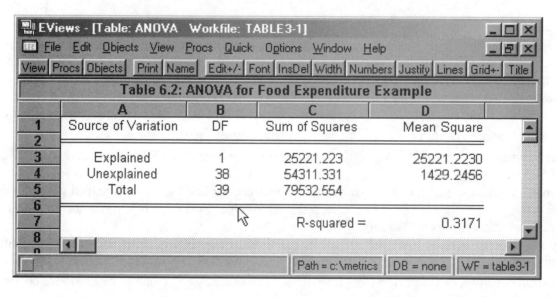

Much of the information provided in the ANOVA table for the food expenditure example is also available in the standard EViews equation object view, which we present for equation (3.3.9) below.

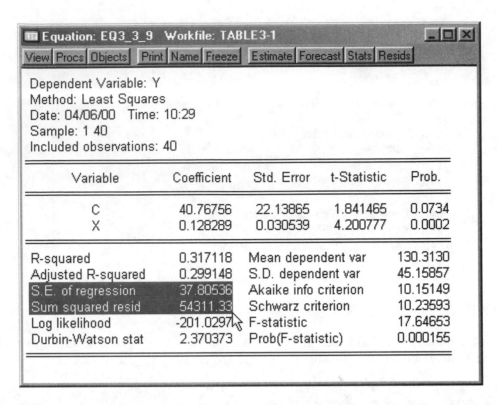

- The coefficient of determination, or R^2, which measures the proportion of variation in the dependent variable, y, that is explained by the regression, is the first regression statistic reported under the coefficient table. For the food expenditure example, $R^2 = 0.32$, indicating 32% of the variation in weekly food expenditures is explained by variations in weekly income.
- We have highlighted the "**S.E. of regression**", which is EViews terminology for the standard error of the regression, $\sqrt{SSE/(T-2)}$. Squaring this quantity gives us our sample estimate of the unexplained variance or "mean square error", from the ANOVA table we created above. That is, $(37.80536)^2 = 1429.2456$.
- Immediately below the standard error of the regression, we find the "**Sum squared resid**", which the text refers to as the error sum of squares, *SSE*. This value, 54311.33, is found in the unexplained sum of squares cell of the ANOVA table above.
- We can reconstruct the total sum of squares, *SST* from the EViews statistic "**S.D. dependent var**", which means the sample standard deviation of the dependent variable, y. The formula for this standard deviation is $\sqrt{SST/(T-1)}$. If we square this quantity and multiply by (T−1) we obtain *SST*.
- In our food expenditure example, (T−1) = 39 and the required calculation is 39*(45.15857)^2 = 79532.554, which is reported in the ANOVA table in the cell labeled total sum of squares.
- As a practical matter, since all of the ANOVA table measures are closely correlated to their EViews regression output counterparts compared above, the EViews regression output provides all of the statistical information required by researchers, albeit in a slightly different form.

6.2   The Effects of Scaling the Data

To replicate the effects of scaling the weekly income data, x_t, open the workfile *table3-1.wf1* and type the following command in the EViews command window:

```
genr xstar = x/100                    scales the income variable x
equation x100.ls y c xstar            estimates the new equation x100 using xstar
```

These commands create the following regression output for the equation named **x100**. Note two things about these commands.

1. In the main workfile window we could have clicked the **genr** button, and filled in the dialog box with the equation xstar = x/100 to create the variable **xstar**. Instead we have simply issued a command directly.

2. We have presented a new way for you to obtain regression results. Instead of using the menu items **Quick/Estimate Equation**, etc., we have issued the command equation x100.ls y c xstar. The "**x100.ls**" tells EViews that you want a least squares (**ls**) regression and for the resulting equation to be named **x100**. The variable specification is as usual, with the dependent variable y, the intercept term c and the independent variable x. The result is

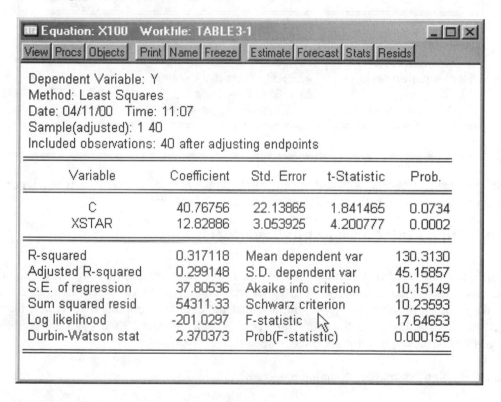

Note that, as in your text, the constant is unchanged with a value of 40.77. The estimate slope coefficient b_2, and its associated standard error $se(b_2)$, are each now 100 times their estimated values contained in equation (3.3.9). This implies that the t-statistic associated with the null hypothesis H_0: $b_2 = 0$, will be unchanged, since $t = b_2/se(b_2) = 100b_2/100se(b_2)$. Indeed, the t-statistic reported above, 4.2, is the same as the one reported in the equation (3.3.9) regression output.

Next, we conduct a scaling experiment to see the effects of measuring food expenditures, y_t, in cents rather than dollars. This experiment requires the creation of a new variable, $y_t^* = 100\ y_t$. We enter the following commands in the EViews command window:

```
genr ystar = y*100                    scales the food expenditure variable y
equation y100.ls ystar c x            estimates the new equation y100 using ystar
```

These commands produce the following EViews regression output from the equation named **y100**:

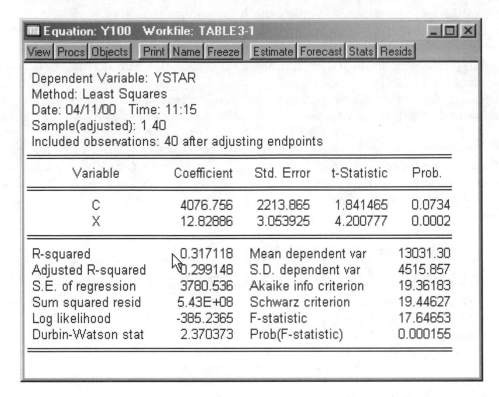

As described in result (R6.9), both estimated coefficients b_1 and b_2 are 100 times larger than their counterparts from equation (3.3.9), as are their estimated standard errors.

6.3   Choosing a Functional Form: Empirical Issues

A new example is introduced in Chapter 6.3.3 of *UE/2*. We will create a new workfile for this example. We have not done this since Chapter 1, so it is a good time to practice. Open the data file *y1y4.dat* to examine the data before proceeding. You will note that the data file contains 5 variables, but no variable names. The first 3 variables are defined in *Exercise 6.12*. The 4th and 5th variables are defined in the text to be wheat yield in Greenough Shire and time, respectively.

In EViews click on **New/Workfile**. A dialog box opens.

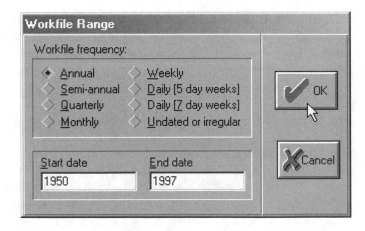

Indicate that the data are annual and the starting and ending years. Click **OK**. Save this workfile with the name **WA-wheat**, where the WA is for Western Australia. Click on **File/Import/Read Text-Lotus-Excel**. In the dialog box that opens, select the data file ***y1y4.dat***. You can obtain this file from your instructor or the web site for *UE/2*.

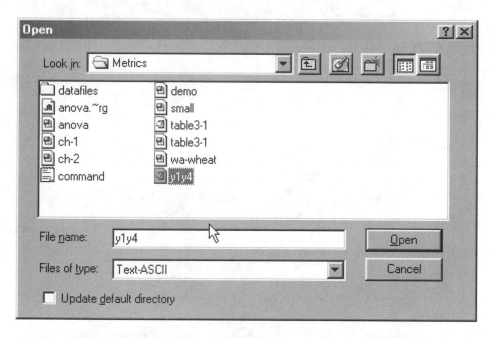

In the next window, name the variables **north, chap, mull, green** and **time**. Click **OK**.

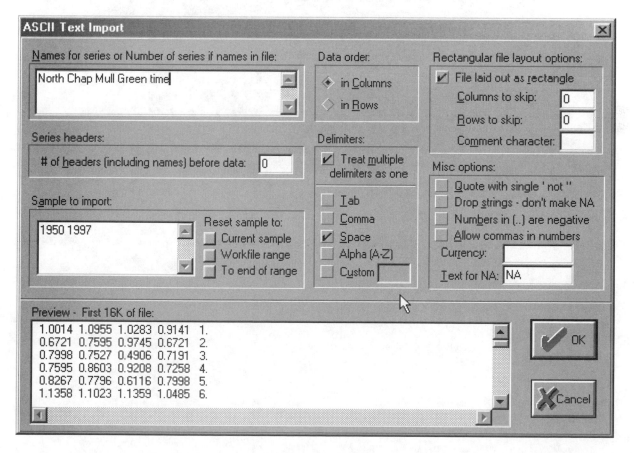

In the resulting workfile, click **Quick/Graph**.   Plot the yield from Greenough Shire against time by entering **time** and **green** in the dialog box.

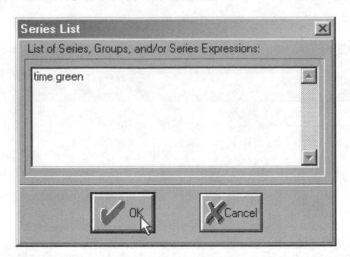

Select **Scatter Diagram** in the subsequent **Graph** dialog box.

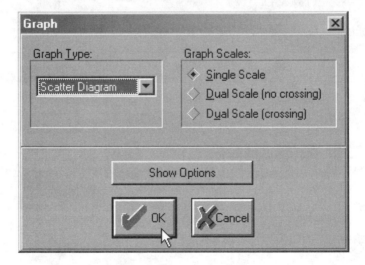

The resulting graph is Figure 6.4 in *UE/2*.

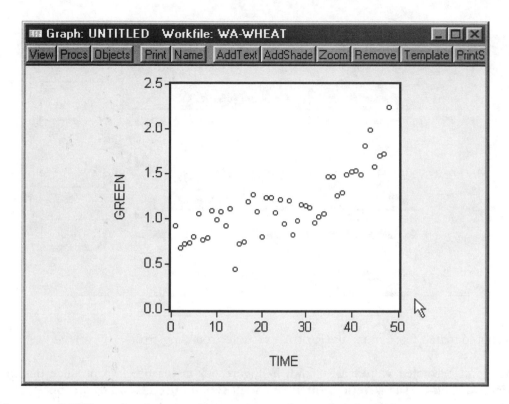

A handy feature of EViews is that graphs can be easily copied into documents.   To do so, click **Edit/Copy** on the main workfile toolbar. A dialog box opens.

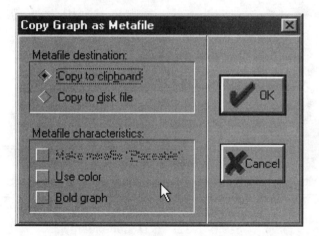

You can copy the graph to the Windows clipboard, or save it as an image file. If you have a color printer, you can save it in color. Click **OK**. Now open a new document and paste the image into it. Before you do this you may want to edit the figure to include a title, or other explanations. To do so, use the buttons in the graph window.

Now estimate a simple regression with wheat yield as the dependent variable and time as the independent variable. Click **Quick/Estimate Equation**. Enter **green c time** in the resulting dialog box and click **OK**.

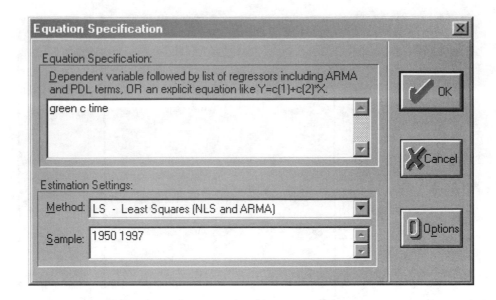

The results should match those in result (R6.10), except for rounding error.

The residuals and predicted values are shown in Figure 6.5 in the text. To produce this graph, in the equation window, click on **View/Actual,Fitted,Residual/Actual,Fitted,Residual Graph**.

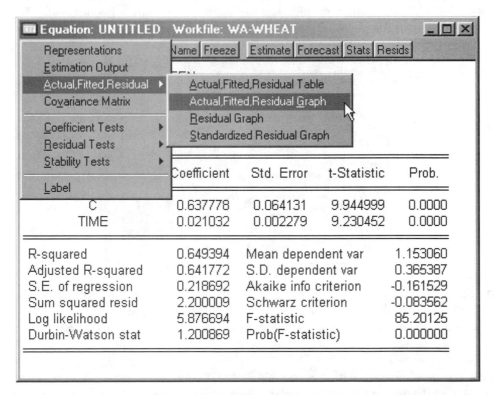

The bar graph of the residuals in Figure 6.6 is obtained by double clicking the **RESID** vector in the workfile window. This variable always contains the residuals from the most recent regression.

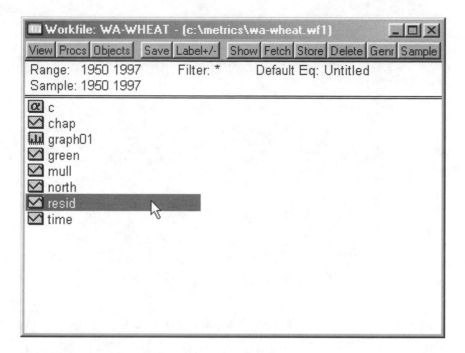

In the spreadsheet view that opens, click on **View/Bar Graph**.

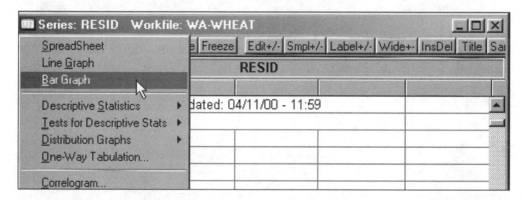

To estimate the equation in result (R6.11) we must create the variable

$$z_t^3 = x_t^3 / 1,000,000$$

where x_t is **time**. Click on **genr** in the main workfile window. In the resulting dialog box define the desired variable as

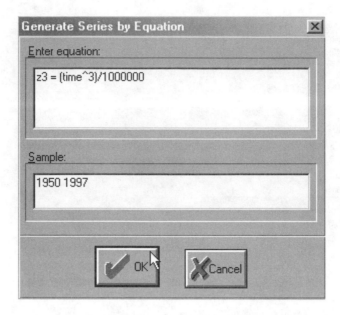

To estimate the equation, click on **Quick/Estimate Equation**. Fill in the dialog box as shown below, and click **OK**.

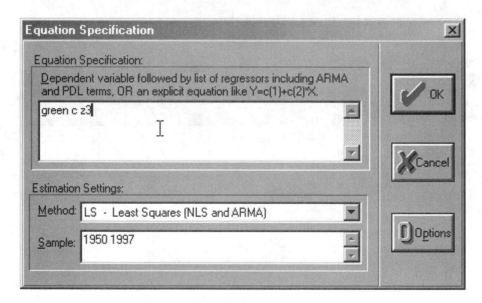

6.4   Are the Residuals Normally Distributed?

To create a histogram and Jarque-Bera statistic for testing the normality of the residuals from the food expenditure example, in workfile *table3-1.wf1*, double-click on the equation object **eq3_3_9** and from its toolbar, click **Estimate** and then **OK**.   Since the workfile series RESID contains the least squares residuals from the most recent regression, we re-estimated equation (3.3.9) to ensure that the series RESID contains the appropriate residuals.

Next, we double-click on the series **RESID** and from the series object toolbar select **View/Descriptive Statistics/Histogram and Stats**.

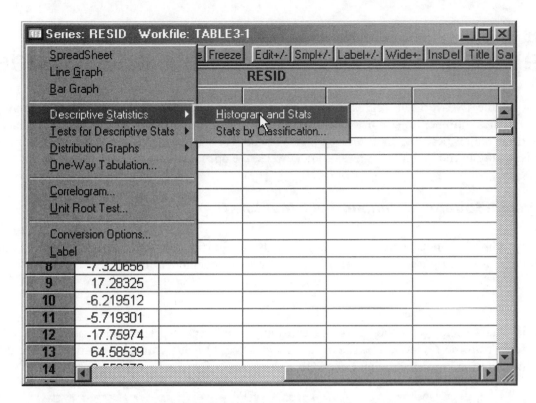

This procedure produces the histogram of the food expenditure equation residuals and the Jarque-Bera statistic found in Figure 6.7 of the text.

For the Jarque-Bera test of normality, we need the 5% critical value from a χ^2 distribution with 2 degrees of freedom. We can use the EViews built-in calculator to obtain this value by typing the following command into the EViews command window:

=@qchisq(.95,2)

The result of this calculation is displayed in the status line at the bottom of the EViews main window.

Scalar = 5.99146454711

As described in the text, since the Jarque-Bera statistic 1.077, is less than the χ^2 critical value, 5.99, we fail to reject the null hypothesis that the residuals are normally distributed. Alternatively, we make the same decision by inspecting the *p*-value. Since the *p*-value, 0.584, is greater than our chosen level of significance, 0.05, we fail to reject the null hypothesis of normality.

Chapter 7 The Multiple Regression Model

While the simple two-variable regression model is useful for learning about regression techniques and indeed valid in a number of empirical contexts, most economic processes have multiple determinants. Hence, we introduce here the multiple regression model. To begin our consideration of estimation and hypothesis testing in the multiple regression framework, we open the workfile *hamburger.wf1*.

7.1　Least Squares Estimation of a Multiple Regression Model

We specify a model of sales revenue for the hamburger chain that depends on price and advertising expenditures. Our multiple regression specification for this model in list form is

tr c p a

Here, tr is total weekly revenue, c is the constant, p is weekly price, and a is weekly advertising expenditure. From the EViews workfile menubar, we select **Quick/Estimate Equation**. In the dialog box we enter the equation specification and click **OK**.

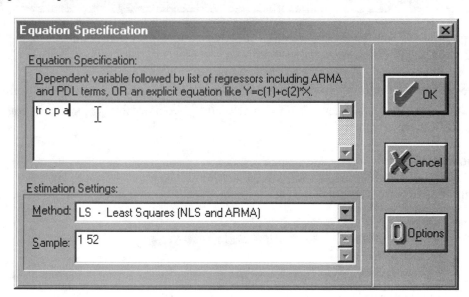

We name the resulting equation object output Result_7_1, as shown below:

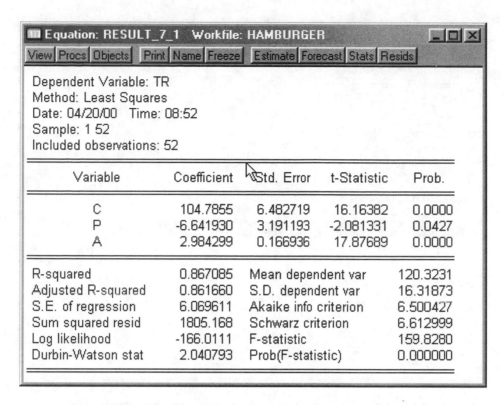

Dependent Variable: TR
Method: Least Squares
Date: 04/20/00   Time: 08:52
Sample: 1 52
Included observations: 52

Variable	Coefficient	Std. Error	t-Statistic	Prob.
C	104.7855	6.482719	16.16382	0.0000
P	-6.641930	3.191193	-2.081331	0.0427
A	2.984299	0.166936	17.87689	0.0000

R-squared	0.867085	Mean dependent var	120.3231
Adjusted R-squared	0.861660	S.D. dependent var	16.31873
S.E. of regression	6.069611	Akaike info criterion	6.500427
Sum squared resid	1805.168	Schwarz criterion	6.612999
Log likelihood	-166.0111	F-statistic	159.8280
Durbin-Watson stat	2.040793	Prob(F-statistic)	0.000000

These estimation results match Table 7.2 in *UE/2*. For details on the interpretation of the coefficients in this multiple regression framework, refer to the text.

7.2   *Simple Prediction*

To use the model for prediction of total revenue when weekly price is $2 per hamburger and weekly advertising expenditure is $10,000, select **View/Representations** from the equation's toolbar and highlight the equation presented under **Substituted Coefficients**.

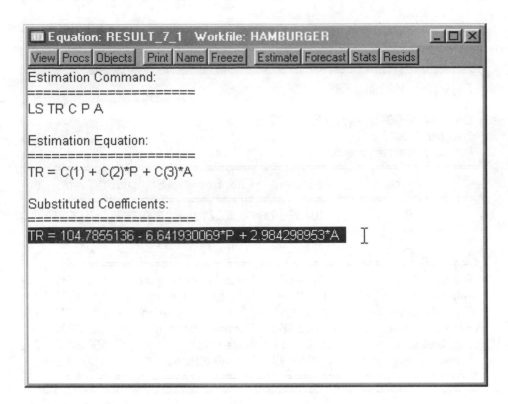

Copy the highlighted text into the EViews command window and edit it to include the assumed values of price (P) and advertising expenditures (A).

Note: It is important to change the name of the variable on the left-hand side of the equals sign to avoid writing over your dependent variable (TR). In fact, we are not creating a series with this command, but rather a scalar, or constant. We choose to call our new scalar **R_7_4**, to reflect the *UE/2* equation number. Our command looks as follows:

scalar R_7_4 = 104.7855136 - 6.641930069*2 + 2.984298953*10

Note that the execution of this command results in a permanent scalar number being created in our workfile. It can be recovered at any time by double-clicking on the following symbol.

r_7_4

This displays the scalar result in the status line at the bottom left-hand corner of the EViews main window.

Scalar R_7_4 = 121.344642992

7.3   Estimation of the Error Variance

Econometric researchers are keenly interested in the variance of the error term, σ^2, and EViews routinely reports its square root, σ, as the "S.E. of regression" after every estimation. In the hamburger chain equation output, $\sigma = 6.096$. We can simply square this value to recover the error variance, σ^2, that is, $(6.096)^2 = 36.84$. To compute this value ourselves, we can use the results that EViews stores after each regression estimation. Some of these are:

@ncoef	total number of estimated coefficients
@regobs	number of observations in regression
@sddep	standard deviation of the dependent variable
@se	standard error of the regression
@ssr	sum of squared residuals

We provide the following commands to reproduce the various steps required to compute the error variance according to equation (7.2.6) in *UE/2*.

```
coef(5) sigma2
sigma2(1) = @ssr
sigma2(2) = @regobs
sigma2(3) = @ncoef
sigma2(4) = @ssr/(@regobs-@ncoef)
sigma2(5) = (@ssr/(@regobs-@ncoef))^.5
```

The fourth and fifth elements of sigma2 are σ^2, and σ, respectively. Note that σ can be recovered using the stored result @se.

7.4   The Variances and Covariances of the Least Squares Estimators

We are interested in the reliability of our least squares estimates, and the variance-covariance matrix provides us with a convenient summary presentation of the relevant variances for assessing reliability. In EViews, the variance-covariance matrix is a particular view of an equation object. To produce the variance-covariance matrix for the hamburger chain problem as found in Table 7.3 of the text, from the regression output window, select **View/Covariance Matrix**

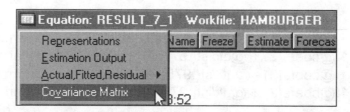

The covariance matrix is

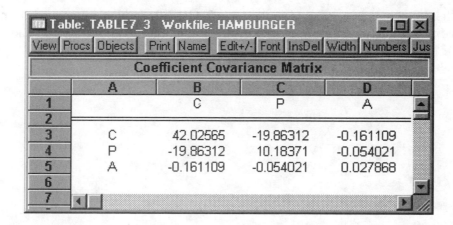

We create a table named **TABLE7_3** by **freezing** the view of the variance-covariance matrix. In this table, the elements on the diagonal are the variances of the least squares estimators, b_1, b_2, b_3, and the off-diagonal elements are the covariances of the least squares estimators. For example, the number 10.18371 is the variance of the coefficient b_2, $var(b_2)$, on the price variable in our multiple regression model. The number −0.054021 is the covariance between b_2 and b_3, $cov(b_2,b_3)$, the coefficients on the price and advertising expenditures variables, respectively

7.5   *Interval Estimation*

To estimate 95% confidence intervals for β_2 and β_3 use the stored regression results. The elements we need are

- @coefs(i)   coefficient i, where i is given by the order in which the coefficients appear in the representations view
- @stderrs(i)   standard error for coefficient i

Also, from Chapter 5.1 of this book, the function **@qtdist**,

- The quantile function `@qtdist(p,v)` computes the **critical value** of a *t*-random variable with **v** degrees of freedom such that probability **p** falls to the left of it. For example, if we specify *tcrit=@qtdist*(.975,38), then

$$P\left[t_{(38)} \leq tcrit\right] = .975 .$$

Enter the following commands in the EViews command window:

```
coef(4) confint                                                        Creates a storage vector
confint(1) = result_7_1.@coefs(2) - @qtdist(.975,49)*result_7_1.@stderrs(2)    β₂ lower
confint(2) = result_7_1.@coefs(2) + @qtdist(.975,49)*result_7_1.@stderrs(2)    β₂ upper
confint(3) = result_7_1.@coefs(3) - @qtdist(.975,49)*result_7_1.@stderrs(3)    β₃ lower
confint(4) = result_7_1.@coefs(3) + @qtdist(.975,49)*result_7_1.@stderrs(3)    β₃ upper
```

The results of these commands are found in the table **TABLE01**, which we created from the coefficient storage vector **confint** by freezing the view and adding a title, numerical formatting, and the labels found in column A.

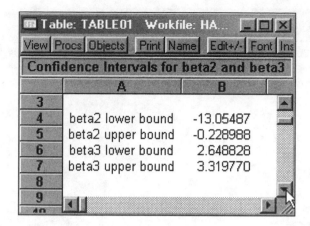

Note that the 95% confidence interval estimate for β_2, [-13.05, -0.23], is very wide, indicating that the point estimate for β_2 is somewhat unreliable. Regarding β_3, our confidence interval is reasonably narrow, [2.65, 3.32], due to the smaller sampling variability associated with its standard error.

7.6 Hypothesis Testing for a Single Coefficient

7.6.1 Using the Program TTEST

In this section we demonstrate how to use EViews to conduct hypothesis tests for individual coefficients in the multiple regression model. Specifically, we show how to formulate and carry out tests of significance and more general hypothesis tests using the t-statistic.

To generate the hypothesis tests contained in section 7.5 of *UE/2*, we employ an EViews program **ttest** designed to format the table according to the standard presented in the text. This EViews program is available for download from the textbook website at: **http://www.wiley.com/college/hill**. To use the program, you must have downloaded **ttest** from the website and copied it into a suitable subdirectory on your hard drive. From the EViews menu bar, select **File/Open/Program**

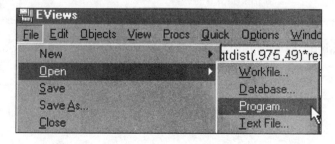

Select the EViews program **ttest** from the appropriate subdirectory.

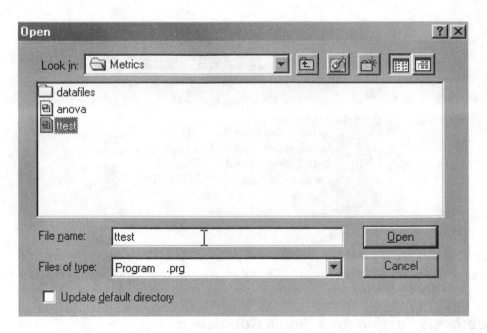

For the test of significance of the weekly price coefficient, β_2, make sure the workfile statement refers to the appropriate workfile, in this case **hamburger**. Then set the coefficient number **!k** = 2, the null hypothesis value **!h0** = 0, the type of test **!tail** = 2 for a two-tailed test, and finally, the chosen significance level **!sig** = .05.

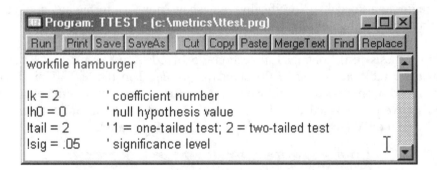

To produce an EViews table of the significance test for β_2, click on **Run** from the program's toolbar and then click **OK**. If the **Program name or path:** does not automatically appear in the dialog box, enter it.

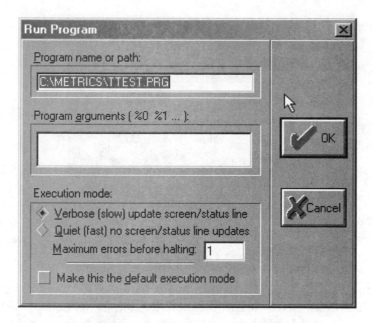

The program creates the following tabular results:

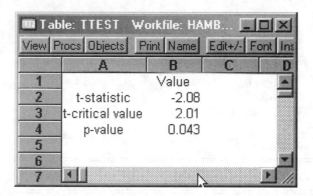

Here we reject the null hypothesis that price has no effect on weekly total hamburger revenue since the absolute value of our computed t-statistic, 2.08, exceeds the t-critical value, 2.01. We reach the same conclusion by noting that our computed *p*-value, 0.043, is less than our chosen level of significance, $\alpha = 0.05$.

Note: To save the results from this hypothesis test, we must provide a different name for the resulting table to prevent it from being written over during subsequent hypothesis tests. We have saved this table in the workfile **hamburger** as **sigb2**.

Next, we employ the same program **ttest** to conduct a significance test for the coefficient on weekly advertising expenditure, β_2. The following control variable settings are appropriate for this test: **!k** = 3, **!h0** = 0, **!tail** = 2, and **!sig** = .05. We save the results of this test in a table renamed **sigb3**

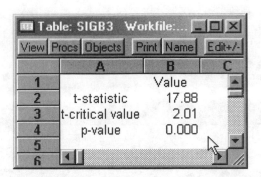

Our conclusion, once again, is to reject the null hypothesis that weekly advertising expenditures have no effect on weekly hamburger revenues since our computed t-statistic, 17.88, exceeds the critical t value, 2.01. Alternatively, our *p*-value is essentially zero, which is less than our chosen significance level, $\alpha = 0.05$, so we reach the same conclusion and reject the null hypothesis.

Referring once again to the regression output from the equation object, we note that the t-statistics and their associated *p*-values constructed under the null hypothesis associated with tests of statistical significance are routinely reported in EViews. We can draw conclusions about statistical significance directly from the EViews equation output, without having to run the **ttest** program.

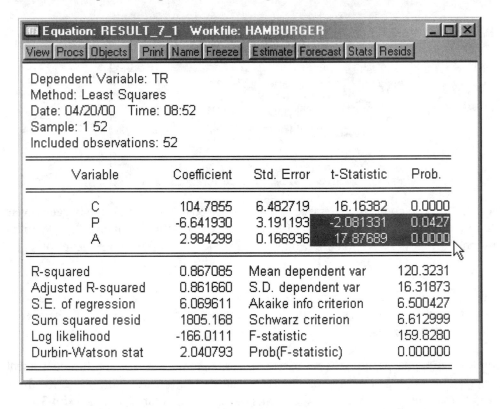

For more general one- and two-tailed hypothesis tests, however, it is useful to have a program such as **ttest** to perform the statistical calculations. For example, we might want to know if the demand curve facing the hamburger chain is elastic. As discussed in the text, such a conjecture involves the coefficient on price, β_2. Recall from microeconomic theory that total revenue will fall if the firm raises its price when demand is elastic, as the percentage decline in quantity demanded exceeds the percentage increase in price. This is a statement about the expected value of β_2, namely if $\beta_2 < 0$, when the weekly hamburger price rises, total hamburger revenue falls. This is an example of a one-tailed test and with the appropriate control variable settings we can use our **ttest** program to provide us with the relevant statistics to draw an inference about β_2.

The appropriate control variable settings in **ttest** are:

    !k = 2
    !h0 = 0
    !tail = 1
    !sig = .05.

We save the results of this test in a table renamed **ttestb2**.

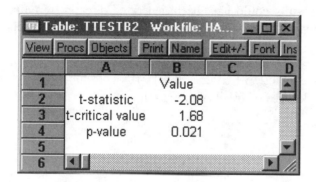

Our decision is to reject the null hypothesis that demand is unit elastic or inelastic in favor of the alternative that demand is elastic. We draw this inference because the absolute value of the t-statistic, 2.08, exceeds the t-critical value, 1.68. Alternatively, our computed p-value, $0.021 < 0.05$, our chosen level of significance, hence we reject the null hypothesis that demand is not elastic.

The final hypothesis test presented in this chapter regards the sufficiency of total hamburger revenue increases to cover increased weekly advertising expenditures. This test concerns β_3.

The appropriate settings for the control variables in the **ttest** program are:

    !k = 3
    !h0 = 1
    !tail = 1
    !sig = .05.

We save the results of this test in a table renamed **ttestb3**.

We reject the null hypothesis that total hamburger revenue increases will be insufficient to cover the increased advertising expenditures since our computed t-statistic, 11.89, exceeds the t-critical value, 1.68. We reach the same conclusion by examining the *p*-value, which is essentially zero and therefore less than our chosen level of significance, $\alpha = 0.05$.

7.6.2 Computing the Tests Directly

These four hypothesis test results could have been generated directly by typing commands in the EViews command window. To compute the *p*-values, we need the function **@ctdist**, which we introduced in Chapter 5.1 of this manual.

- The CDF is given by the function **@ctdist(x,v)**. This function returns the **probability** that a *t*-random variable with **v** degrees of freedom falls to the left of **x**. That is,

$$@ctdist(x,v) = P\left[\, t_{(v)} \leq x \,\right] .$$

Type in the following four sets of commands into the EViews command window:

```
coef(3) b2sigtest                                          Creates a storage vector
b2sigtest(1) = Result_7_1.@coefs(2)/Result_7_1.@stderrs(2)  t-statistic
b2sigtest(2) = @qtdist(.975,49)                             critical value t_c
b2sigtest(3) = 2*(1-@ctdist(abs(b2sigtest(1)),49))          p-value


coef(3) b3sigtest                                          Creates a storage vector
b3sigtest(1) = Result_7_1.@coefs(3)/Result_7_1.@stderrs(3)  t-statistic
b3sigtest(2) = @qtdist(.975,49)                             critical value t_c
b3sigtest(3) = 2*(1-@ctdist(abs(b3sigtest(1)),49))          p-value


coef(3) b2ttest                                           Creates a storage vector
b2ttest(1) = Result_7_1.@coefs(2)/Result_7_1.@stderrs(2)   t-statistic
b2ttest(2) = @qtdist(.95,49)                                critical value t_c
b2ttest(3) = 1-@ctdist(abs(b2ttest(1)),49)                  p-value


coef(3) b3ttest                                           Creates a storage vector
b3ttest(1) = (Result_7_1.@coefs(3) - 1)/Result_7_1.@stderrs(3)  t-statistic
b3ttest(2) = @qtdist(.95,49)                                critical value t_c
b3ttest(3) = 1-@ctdist(abs(b3ttest(1)),49)                  p-value
```

7.7   *Measuring Goodness of Fit*

The goodness of fit measures R^2 and adjusted-R^2 are given in the basic EViews regression output.

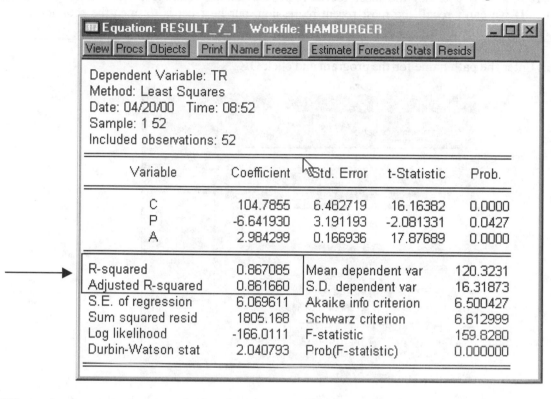

EViews does not report an analysis of variance table as such, but the program **anova** will do the job. Also, we want to make sure you can carry out these calculations directly.

7.7.1 Using the ANOVA Program

To assess goodness of fit in the hamburger chain model, we open the program **anova** to examine the analysis of variance ANOVA table. We first used this program in Chapter 6.1 of this manual. From the EViews menubar, select **File/Open/Program...**, and select the EViews program **anova** from the appropriate subdirectory.

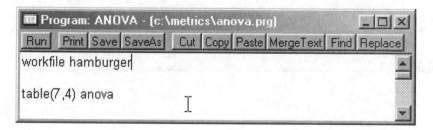

> **Important note:** The **anova** program is designed to produce an ANOVA table for the most recent regression.   Here we want the ANOVA table for the regression model found in equation object Result_7_1.   If Result_7_1 is not the most recent regression model estimated, we will get a different ANOVA table.   If we can't recall the most recent regression, our best bet is to open the equation object we want and re-estimate the model.

Click on **Run**. Enter the path name for the program and click **OK**.

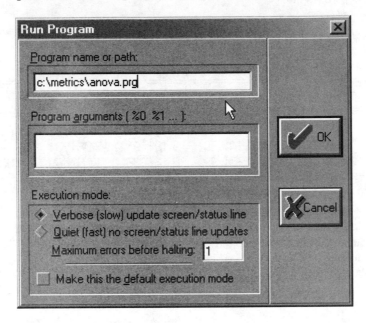

The result is,

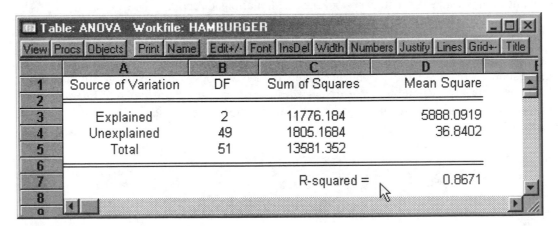

7.7.2 Directly Computing the Goodness of Fit Measures

To compute the R^2 and adjusted-R^2, we use the stored regression results. In addition to the stored results we have already used, we make use of

> **@sddep**   standard deviation of the dependent variable

This value is computed as

$$\sigma_y = \sqrt{\frac{\sum(y_t - \bar{y})^2}{T-1}} = \sqrt{\frac{SST}{T-1}}$$

This value can be used to recover the "total" sum of squares, *SST*, which appears in the goodness of fit values.

> r2 = 1 - @ssr/((@regobs-1)*(@sddep)^2)
> r2adj = 1 - (@se/@sddep)^2

where **@ssr** = the error or "unexplained" sum of squares, 1805.1684, and (@regobs-1)*(@sddep)^2 = the total sum of squares, 13581.352 from the ANOVA table shown above. The adjusted R^2 is simply the square of the ratio of the standard error of the regression, **@se**, to the sample standard deviation of the dependent variable, **@sddep**. For the hamburger chain problem, $R^2 = 0.867$ and adjusted-$R^2 = 0.8617$.

Chapter 8 Further Inference in the Multiple Regression Model

In this chapter we continue working with the hamburger chain data found in Table 7.1. Our task is to use EViews to conduct single and joint coefficient hypothesis tests and to incorporate nonsample information.

8.1 *The F-test*

8.1.1 Constructing the *F*-Statistic

The *F*-statistic given in *UE/2* equation (8.1.3).

$$F = \frac{(SSE_R - SSE_U)/J}{SSE_U/(T-K)}$$

(8.1.3)

To compute this statistic we need:
i. SSE_U = the sum of squared errors for the model being tested
ii. SSE_R = the *SSE* for the restricted model, in which we assume the hypothesis is true
iii. *J* is the number of hypotheses being tested.
iv. *T* is the number of sample observations
v. *K* is thenumber of parameters in the original model (including the intercept)

We will use the *F*-test to test the null hypothesis $H_0 : \beta_2 = 0$ against $H_1 : \beta_2 \neq 0$.

- Open the workfile *hamburger.wf1*, which we used in Chapter 7, and click on **Quick/Estimate Equation** and type in the total revenue equation making sure to include the intercept (**C** in EViews notation). Click **OK**.

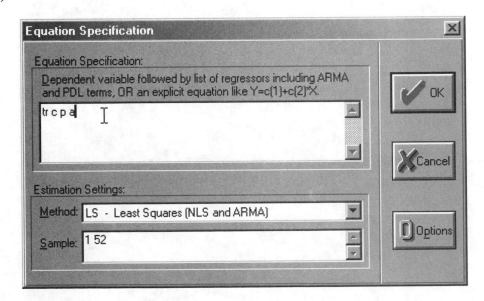

From the stored results, we must save the sum of squared errors.

coef(6) ftest	**coef vector**
ftest(1)=result_7_1.@ssr	**SSE_U**
ftest(2)=result_7_1.@regobs-result_7_1.@ncoef	**T-K**

Now estimate the "restricted" model, assuming the null hypothesis is true.

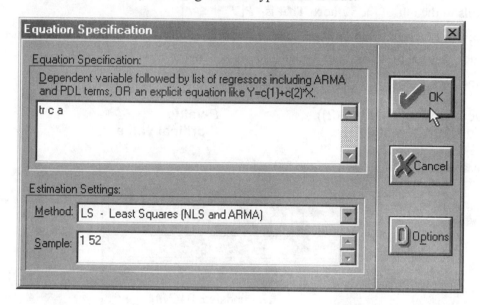

Name the resulting object "**Restrict1**".

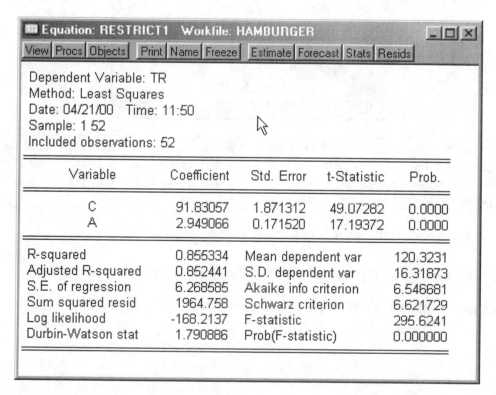

Dependent Variable: TR
Method: Least Squares
Date: 04/21/00   Time: 11:50
Sample: 1 52
Included observations: 52

Variable	Coefficient	Std. Error	t-Statistic	Prob.
C	91.83057	1.871312	49.07282	0.0000
A	2.949066	0.171520	17.19372	0.0000

R-squared	0.855334	Mean dependent var	120.3231
Adjusted R-squared	0.852441	S.D. dependent var	16.31873
S.E. of regression	6.268585	Akaike info criterion	6.546681
Sum squared resid	1964.758	Schwarz criterion	6.621729
Log likelihood	-168.2137	F-statistic	295.6241
Durbin-Watson stat	1.790886	Prob(F-statistic)	0.000000

Save the sum of squared errors and compute the *F*-statistic.

ftest(3)=restrict1.@ssr	**SSE_R**
ftest(4)=(ftest(3)-ftest(1))/(ftest(1)/ftest(2))	**F-stat**

In order to compute *p*-values and critical values for the *F*-statistic we need to use two EViews functions.

- **@cfdist(x,v1,v2)** computes the probability that the *F*-random variable with v1 and v2 degrees of freedom falls to the **left** of the value x. That is, $P\left[F_{v_1,v_2} \le x\right]$

- **@qfdist(p,v1,v2)** computes the critical value F_c from the *F*-distribution with v1 and v2 degrees of freedom such that the probability to the **left** of F_c is *p*. That is, $p = P\left[F_{v_1,v_2} \le F_c\right]$

Using these functions,

ftest(5)=1-@cfdist(ftest(4),1,ftest(2))	**P-value**
ftest(6)=@qfdist(.95,1,ftest(2))	**F-critical value**

Freezing the result, and editing, we have the following:

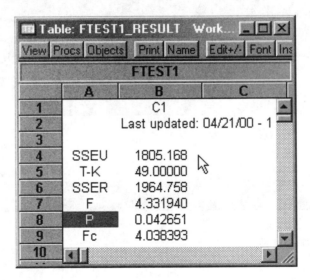

> **Note:** We have "programmed" the calculations in EViews. Given the results of the unrestricted and restricted regressions, the F-statistic value could be computed on a calculator and the critical value looked up (approximately) in the F-tables at the end of *UE/2*. The advantage of using EViews is that we can compute the *p*-value and the exact critical value.

8.1.2 Using EViews Coefficient Tests

EViews makes using the *F*-test very simple. Return to the regression output object **Result_7_1**.

- Click on **View/Coefficient Tests/Wald-Coefficient Restrictions**, as shown in the next figure.

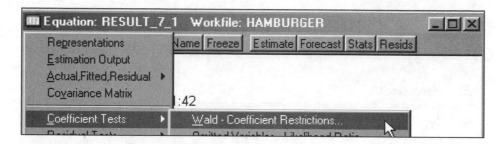

A dialog box opens in which you type in the hypotheses you wish to test. The test is stated in terms of the coefficient number, as shown in the **representations** view of the output

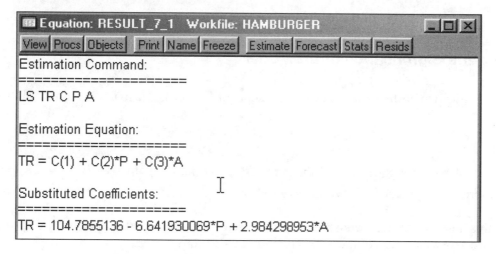

β_2 is c(2). Enter the hypothesis and click **OK**.

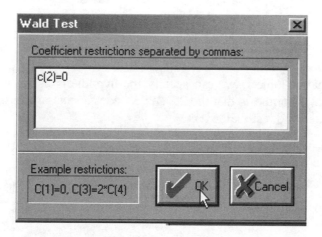

The result is shown in the next figure, which is Table 8.1 in *UE/2*. Ignore the "Chi-square" value. It is an alternative testing procedure which we will not consider.

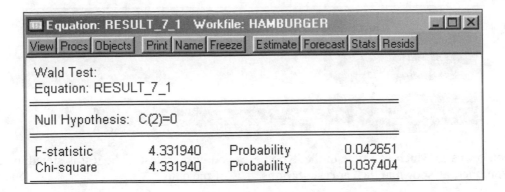

8.2 Testing the Significance of the Model

The overall significance of the model is evaluated using an *F*-test. In the multiple regression model

$$y_t = \beta_1 + \beta_2 x_{t2} + \beta_3 x_{t3} + \cdots + \beta_K x_{tK} + e_t$$

the overall test of model significance is the joint test of the null hypothesis $H_0 : \beta_2 = 0, \beta_3 = 0, \ldots, \beta_K = 0$ against the alternative hypothesis H_1: *at least one* of the β_k is nonzero.

In EViews this test is reported automatically as part of the regression output, in the lower right-hand corner. We are given the value of the test statistic and its *p*-value.

F-statistic	159.8280
Prob(F-statistic)	0.000000

We can also create this value from the ANOVA table output in Chapter 7.7.1 of this manual.

Alternatively, in the estimation object, we can specify the hypothesis as we did in the previous section. We now jointly test the null hypothesis that the 2nd and 3rd coefficients are zero. Multiple hypotheses are separated by commas in the Wald test dialog box.

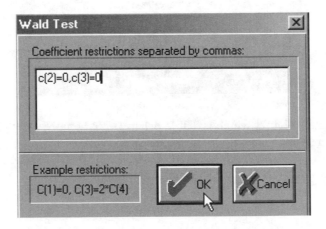

The output is the same as reported in the EViews output.

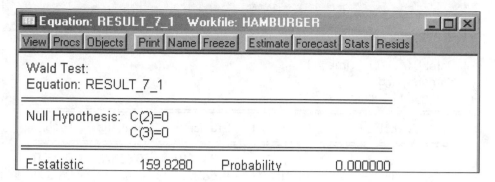

8.3 An Extended Model

The workfile *chap8-3* contains 78 weeks of observations on *tr*, *p* and *a*. To reproduce the results in Result 8.5

- Click on **Quick/Estimate Equation** from the EViews main menu and specify equation (8.4.1), including the advertising squared term A^2. Note the EViews exponentiation character is '^'. Click on **OK**.

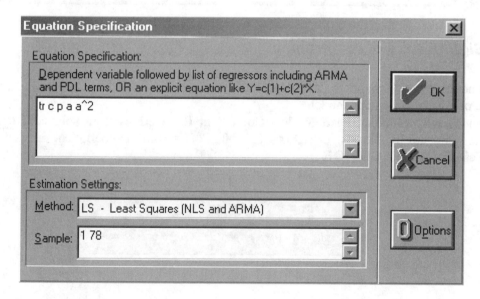

Your results are as follows:

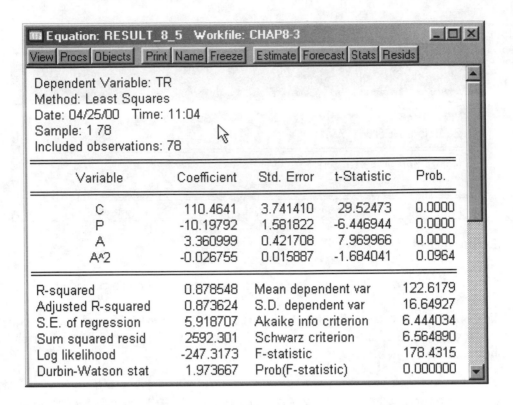

8.4 The Significance of Advertising

Next we generate the F-statistic for the joint test of the hypothesis: H_0: $\beta_3 = 0$, $\beta_4 = 0$ to determine the significance of advertising in our model.

- Click on **View/Coefficient Tests/Wald - Coefficient Restrictions** from your equation's toolbar and enter the joint null hypothesis restrictions **C(3)=0, C(4) = 0** in the coefficient restrictions field of the Wald Test dialog box. Click **OK**.

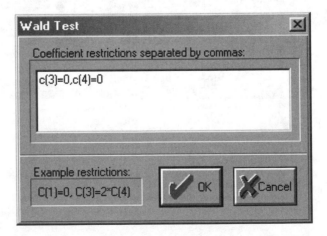

The resulting $F_{(J,T\text{-}K)}$ test statistic has J degrees of freedom in the numerator and $T{-}K$ degrees of freedom in the denominator, where J = the number of coefficient restrictions, T = the number of observations in the sample, and K = the number of estimated coefficients. In this case, $J = 2$, $T = 78$, and $K = 4$.

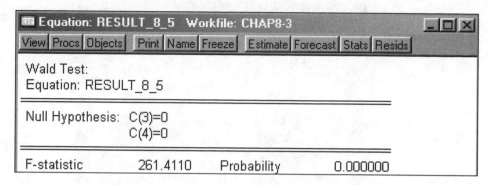

The F-statistic is 261.41 whereas the $F_{(2,74)}$ critical value is 3.12. As your text notes, our conclusion is to reject the null hypothesis that advertising has no statistically significant effect on total revenue in favor of the alternative hypothesis that at least one of the advertising coefficients is non-zero.

The foregoing F-test statistic and F-critical value could also be computed with the following commands typed into the EViews command window:

scalar fstat = ((eq_r.@ssr – eq_u.@ssr)/2)/(eq_u.@ssr/(@regobs – eq_u.@ncoef))
scalar fcrit = @qfdist(.95,2,74)

where
- $tr_t = \beta_1 + \beta_2 p_t + e_t$ is the restricted equation (eq_r)
- $tr_t = \beta_1 + \beta_2 p_t + \beta_3 a_t + \beta_4 a^2_t + e_t$ is the unrestricted equation (eq_u)
- @ssr is the sum of squared errors (*SSE* in *UE/2*),
- @regobs is the number of regression observations (*T* in your textbook)
- @ncoef is the number of estimated coefficients (*K* in your textbook)
- @qfdist$(1-\alpha,v_1,v_2)$ is the upper α percent right tail critical value for the F-distribution with v_1 degrees of freedom in the numerator and v_2 degrees of freedom in the denominator.

Note: To calculate fstat, you must have previously estimated and named both the restricted (eq_r) and unrestricted (eq_u) equations.

8.5 The Optimal Level of Advertising

To compute the F statistic regarding the hypothesis that $40,000 per week is the optimal level of advertising
- Click on **View/Coefficient Tests/Wald - Coefficient Restrictions** from your equation's toolbar, enter the restriction $\beta_3 + 80\beta_4 = 1$, and click **OK**.

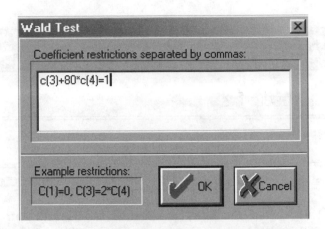

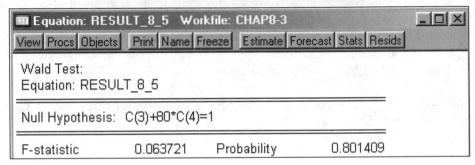

The test statistic follows the F distribution with degrees of freedom in the numerator equal to the number of restrictions ($J = 1$ in this case) and denominator degrees of freedom equal to the number of regression observations less the number of estimated coefficients ($T - K = 74$ in this case). The $F_{(1,74)}$ critical value for $\alpha = .05$ can be computed by typing the following command into the EViews command window:

```
scalar fcrit_ad = @qfdist(.95,1,74)
```

where we name the critical value fcrit_ad so as not to confuse it with the F-critical value calculated earlier.

Since the test statistic value 0.0637 is less than the critical value fcrit_ad = 3.970, we fail to reject the null hypothesis that the optimal level of advertising is \$40,000. Note that this same result is forthcoming from a t-test of the optimal advertising hypothesis. For a single equality hypothesis there is an exact relationship between the F-test and t-test procedures: $t^2 = F$, as explained in Chapter 8.4.2 of *UE/2*. Therefore, either test will produce the same decision. In the optimal advertising case, note that the square root of 0.063721 is 0.252, the t-test statistic reported in result R8.6 in *UE/2*.

8.6 The Optimal Level of Advertising and Price

Next we conduct the F test regarding optimal advertising and price presented in section 8.4.3 of *UE/2*. In EViews,

- Click on **View/Coefficient Tests/Wald - Coefficient Restrictions** from your equation **result_8_5** toolbar and enter the restrictions $\beta_3 + 80\beta_4 = 1$ and $\beta_1 + 2\beta_2 + 40\beta_3 + 1600\beta_4 = 175$ and click **OK.**

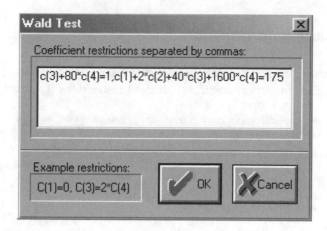

The results of this test are

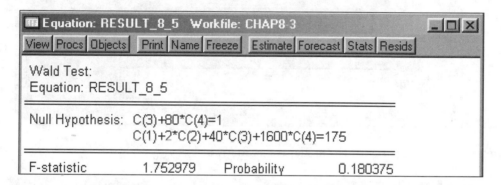

You can compute the $F_{(2,74)}$ critical value for $\alpha = .05$ by typing the following command into the EViews command window:

```
scalar fcrit_ad_price = @qfdist(.95,2,74)
```

Since the F-statistic = 1.75 is less than the F-critical value = 3.12, we fail to reject the null hypothesis that the sample data are consistent with the joint hypothesis that optimal weekly advertising expenditures are $40,000, and at a price of $2 per burger, total revenue will average $175,000 per week.

8.7 The Use of Nonsample Information

To obtain the results presented in R8.8, open the workfile *beer.wf1*, click on **Quick/Estimate Equation**, and type in the Log-Log model, incorporating the coefficient restrictions by direct substitution as follows:

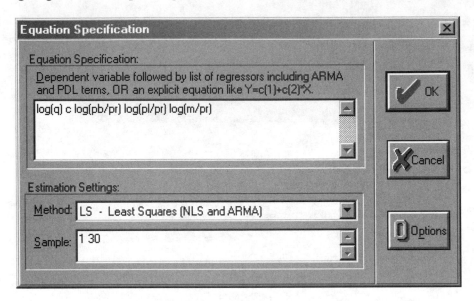

The estimation results for this restricted model are as follows:

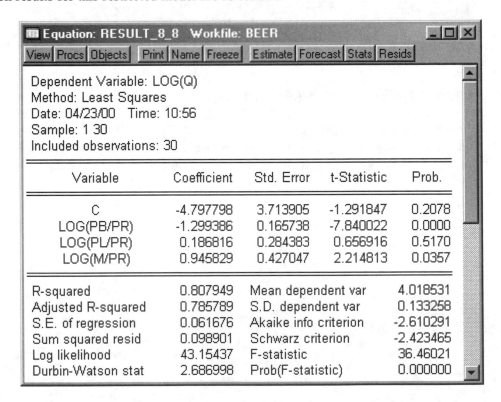

To calculate the value of the coefficient β_4 on $\ln(p_R)$ from the unrestricted model in equation (8.5.5), enter the following command in the EViews command window:

```
scalar beta4 = -c(2) – c(3) – c(4)
```

which produces the result $\beta_4 = 0.1668$, as reported in *UE/2*, below result R8.8. Note that in this command $c(4)$ represents the coefficient 0.9458 on $\ln(m/pR)$ in your restricted model, shown in R8.8.

Chapter 9 Dummy (Binary) Variables

This chapter introduces several important extensions of the multiple regression model that will at once broaden your toolkit of techniques as well as enable you to tackle more sophisticated empirical problems with richly complex interaction effects. The primary tool introduced is the dummy, or category, variable.

9.1 An Example: The University Effect on House Prices

To begin, we open the workfile *utown.wf1*. This workfile contains 1000 observations on the real estate data presented in Table 9.1 in the text. Note the presence of quantitative characteristics, PRICE, SQFT, and AGE, and qualitative characteristics, UTOWN, POOL, and FPLACE. We will also include an interaction term to allow the relationship between PRICE and SQFT to depend on whether or not the house is located near the university. We create the variable USQFT = UTOWN * SQFT by typing the following command into the EViews command window:

genr usqft = utown*sqft

Using equation (9.4.1), note that the inclusion of this interaction term means that the change in PRICE for a one-unit change in SQFT is:

$$\frac{\Delta PRICE}{\Delta SQFT} = \beta_2 + \gamma \times UTOWN.$$

Our hypothesis is that an increase in square footage causes a greater increase in sales price for houses that are close to the university. More formally, we want to test the null hypothesis $H_0: \gamma \leq 0$ against the alternative hypothesis $H_1: \gamma > 0$.

To estimate equation (9.4.1) and obtain the results presented in Table 9.2 in the text, select **Quick/Estimate Equation** from the EViews main menu and specify the equation **PRICE C UTOWN SQFT USQFT AGE POOL FPLACE** in the dialog box. Alternatively, you can type the command **LS PRICE C UTOWN SQFT USQFT AGE POOL FPLACE** in the EViews command window, where **LS** is the EViews command for ordinary least squares.

Our results are as follows:

```
▥ Equation: EQ9_4_1  Workfile: UTOWN                    _ □ ✕
View Procs Objects   Print Name Freeze  Estimate Forecast Stats Resids

Dependent Variable: PRICE
Method: Least Squares
Date: 05/01/00   Time: 15:08
Sample: 1 1000
Included observations: 1000

      Variable     Coefficient   Std. Error   t-Statistic    Prob.

         C          24499.98      6191.721     3.956894      0.0001
       UTOWN        27452.95      8422.582     3.259446      0.0012
        SQFT        76.12177      2.451765     31.04775      0.0000
       USQFT        12.99405      3.320478     3.913307      0.0001
        AGE         -190.0864     51.20461     -3.712291     0.0002
        POOL        4377.163      1196.692     3.657720      0.0003
       FPLACE       1649.176      971.9568     1.696758      0.0901

R-squared           0.870570    Mean dependent var      247655.7
Adjusted R-squared  0.869788    S.D. dependent var      42192.73
S.E. of regression  15225.21    Akaike info criterion   22.10627
Sum squared resid   2.30E+11    Schwarz criterion       22.14062
Log likelihood      -11046.13   F-statistic             1113.183
Durbin-Watson stat  1.986480    Prob(F-statistic)       0.000000
```

Note that the regression R-squared, $R^2 = 0.871$, and F-statistic, $F = 1113.183$, differ slightly from those reported in the text. This is due to differences in rounding routines used by various econometric software packages.

9.2 An Empirical Example of the Chow Test

In this section we investigate the investment strategies of two US corporations, General Electric, and Westinghouse. In particular, we want to know if it is reasonable to impose the same structure on the investment functions for each company, in effect, allowing us to estimate a single investment equation using all 40 observations. To begin, open the workfile *invest.wf1*. The first 20 observations in this workfile comprise GE data; observations 21-40 are the Westinghouse data.

To replicate the results in equation (9.7.6) from the text, select **Quick/Estimate Equation** from the EViews main menu and specify the equation **INV C V K** in the dialog box. Alternatively, we can type the command **LS INV C V K** in the EViews command window. Our results are given in the EViews output below:

```
■■ Equation: EQ9_7_6  Workfile: INVEST                    _□×
View Procs Objects  Print Name Freeze  Estimate Forecast Stats Resids

Dependent Variable: INV
Method: Least Squares
Date: 10/18/99   Time: 14:56
Sample: 1 40
Included observations: 40

      Variable      Coefficient   Std. Error   t-Statistic    Prob.

         C           17.87200     7.024081     2.544390      0.0153
         V           0.015193     0.006196     2.451913      0.0191
         K           0.143579     0.018601     7.718900      0.0000

R-squared              0.809772    Mean dependent var     72.59075
Adjusted R-squared     0.799489    S.D. dependent var     47.24981
S.E. of regression    21.15771    Akaike info criterion   9.013924
Sum squared resid     16563.00    Schwarz criterion       9.140590
Log likelihood        -177.2785   F-statistic            78.75172
Durbin-Watson stat     1.105896   Prob(F-statistic)       0.000000
```

9.2.1 Creating Time Trend Variables

In order to estimate the unrestricted model in equation (9.7.7) in *UE/2* we must create a dummy variable that is 1 for Westinghouse observations and 0 for GE observations. One way to do this is to create an "observation" variable using the @trend function. This function returns a "trend" variable that takes the value 0 for the first observation in the workfile, 1 for the second observation, 2 for the third, and so on. Using this function we can use the **genr** command to create a variable **obs** that identifies the observations from 1 to 40.

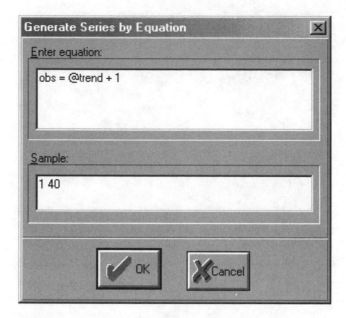

We must add 1 to the trend so that the value of **obs** ranges from 1 to 40.

9.2.2 Using "Logical" Operations

Computer software includes operations that allow us to compare values of variables, or expressions. These are given in the following table.

Expression	Operator	Description
>	greater than	x>y takes the value 1 if X exceeds Y, and 0 otherwise
<	less than	x<y takes the value 1 if Y exceeds X, and 0 otherwise
=	equal to	x=y takes the value 1 if X and Y are equal, and 0 otherwise
<>	not equal to	x<>y takes the value 1 if X and Y are not equal, and 0 if they are equal
<=	less than or equal to	x<=y takes the value 1 if X does not exceed Y, and 0 otherwise
>=	greater than or equal to	x>=y takes the value 1 if Y does not exceed X, and 0 otherwise
and	logical and	x and y takes the value 1 if both X and Y are nonzero, and 0 otherwise
or	logical or	x or y takes the value 1 if either X or Y is nonzero, and 0 otherwise

We can use these expressions when generating dummy variables. The Westinghouse observations are in rows 21-40 of the data. We will create the dummy variable **dv** that is 1 for observations 21-40 and 0 for observations 1-20.

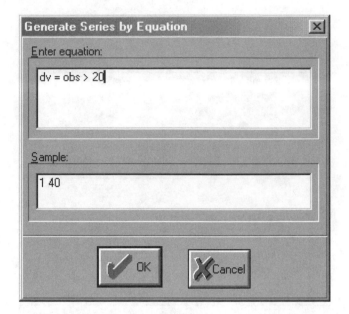

The expression dv = obs > 20 says "return a value of 1 if the statement obs > 20 is true, otherwise return a 0 value. Create this variable and examine its values to verify that we have done what we set out to do.

9.2.3 Estimating and Testing the Unrestricted Model

To estimate equation (9.7.7), click on **Quick/Estimate Equation** and enter the model

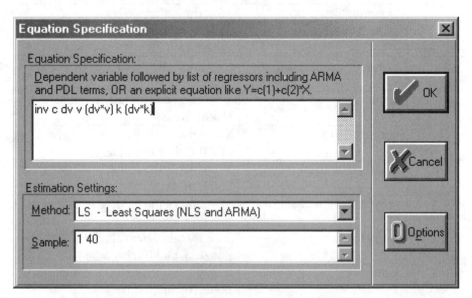

Click **OK**, to obtain the results below, which we have named **EQ9_7_7**.

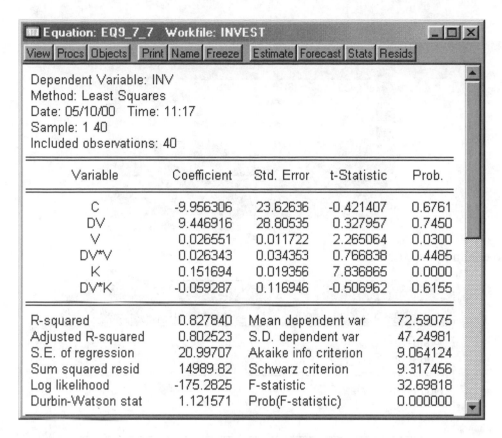

The F-statistic in equation (9.7.8) can be computed from the sums of squared residuals in equations (9.7.6) and (9.7.7). Alternatively we can use EViews' coefficient tests. First, in the window displaying **EQ9_7_7**, click on **View/Representations**. There you will see the coefficient numbers assigned by EViews.

```
Estimation Equation:
=====================
INV = C(1) + C(2)*DV + C(3)*V + C(4)*(DV*V) + C(5)*K + C(6)*(DV*K)
```

Click on **View/Coefficient Tests/Wald-Coefficient Restrictions**. Specify the hypotheses that the coefficients on the dummy variable **dv** and the interaction variables **dv*v** and **dv*k** are zero.

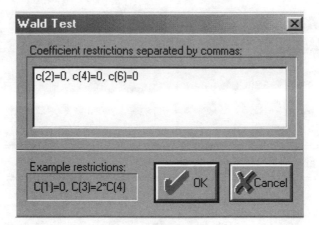

Click **OK** to obtain the test output.

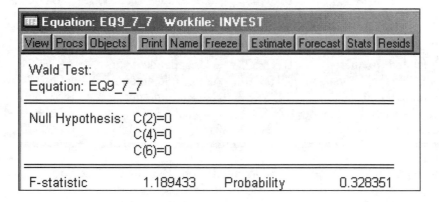

9.2.4 Estimating a Model Using Part of the Sample

With the data stacked together we have estimated the pooled model in equation (9.7.6). What if you wanted to estimate the basic regression just for GE, or just for Westinghouse. This is easily achieved by altering the **Sample** when estimating an equation. Click on **Quick/Estimate Equation**.

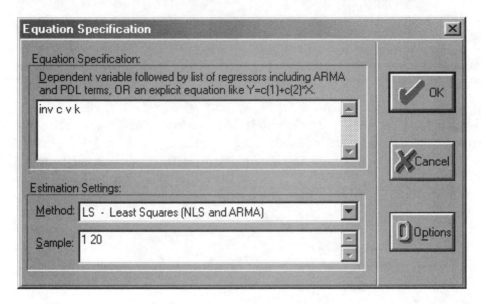

Type in **inv c v k** as the equation specification, but alter the sample to **1 20**. These are the observations for GE, and the resulting estimates will be the investment equation for GE alone. Similarly, for Westinghouse, you would specify the sample to be **21 40**.

9.2.5 Using the EViews Chow Test

The Chow test is of sufficient importance so that EViews has the test procedure "built in." To conduct the Chow test for the equivalence of the two sub-sample investment equations in the single equation you specified above, select **View/Stability Tests/Chow Breakpoint Test** from the toolbar of equation **EQ9_7_6**. Specify the Chow breakpoint to occur at observation 21, the first observation for the Westinghouse data, by entering **21** in the Chow Tests dialog box.

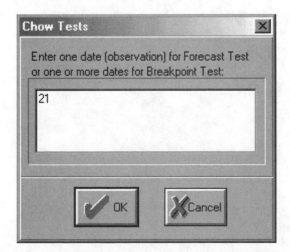

EViews calculates the F statistic presented in equation (9.7.8) of your text.

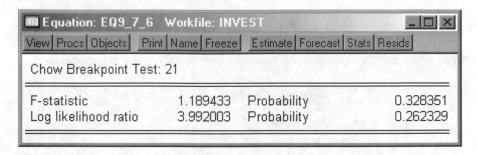

At the 0.05 significance level, the critical F value is 2.8826. Since the $F_{(3,34)}$ statistic, 1.1894 is less than the critical value, 2.8826, we fail to reject the null hypothesis that $\delta_1 = \delta_2 = \delta_3 = 0$, that is, that the coefficients on the slope and intercept dummy variable terms in the model are jointly zero. This statistical evidence suggests that GE and Westinghouse share the same investment equation, which we estimated above as the restricted equation, EQ9_7_6.

Chapter 10: Nonlinear Models

This chapter introduces another important analytical technique employed frequently in the multiple regression framework: interaction terms. We also consider models that are nonlinear in the parameters. Such models have no closed form algebraic solutions for the coefficient estimates so they must be obtained from numerical optimization algorithms that iterate toward a convergence on the "best" estimate.

10.1 Interactions Between Two Continuous Variables

Here we construct a model that allows the effect of changes in one independent variable (X_1) to depend on the level of one of the other independent variables (X_2). For example, we may expect the effect of changes in income (Y) on the demand for PIZZA to depend on AGE. The text uses the PIZZA expenditure data found in Table 10.1 to investigate such a conditional slope model.

To begin, open the workfile *pizza.wf1*. To estimate equation (R10.2) from *UE/2*, select **Quick/Estimate Equation** from the EViews main menu and specify the equation **PIZZA C AGE Y Y*AGE** in the dialog box. Alternatively, type the command **LS PIZZA C AGE Y Y*AGE** in the EViews command window.

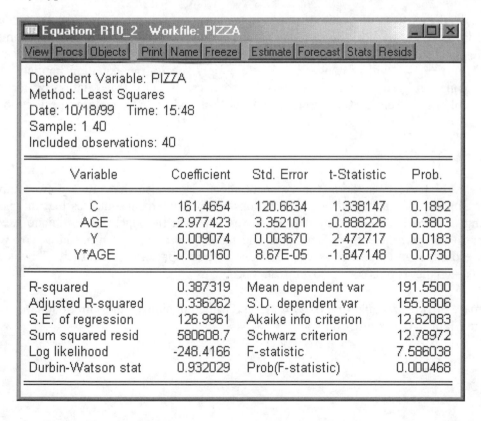

Dependent Variable: PIZZA
Method: Least Squares
Date: 10/18/99   Time: 15:48
Sample: 1 40
Included observations: 40

Variable	Coefficient	Std. Error	t-Statistic	Prob.
C	161.4654	120.6634	1.338147	0.1892
AGE	-2.977423	3.352101	-0.888226	0.3803
Y	0.009074	0.003670	2.472717	0.0183
Y*AGE	-0.000160	8.67E-05	-1.847148	0.0730

R-squared	0.387319	Mean dependent var	191.5500
Adjusted R-squared	0.336262	S.D. dependent var	155.8806
S.E. of regression	126.9961	Akaike info criterion	12.62083
Sum squared resid	580608.7	Schwarz criterion	12.78972
Log likelihood	-248.4166	F-statistic	7.586038
Durbin-Watson stat	0.932029	Prob(F-statistic)	0.000468

To calculate the marginal contribution of AGE to expenditures on PIZZA for individuals with incomes of $25,000 and $90,000, respectively, enter the following commands in the EViews command window:

```
coef(2) mps                                    Creates a storage vector
mps(1) = C(2) + C(4)*25000                     Marginal propensity to spend on pizza
                                               for person with $25,000 income
mps(2) = C(2) + C(4)*90000                     Marginal propensity to spend on pizza
                                               for person with $90,000 income
```

These commands create the storage vector mps in the workfile. We freeze mps as the table R10_3 presented below.

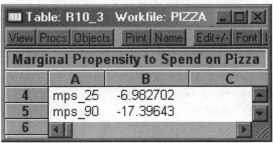

10.2 A Simple Nonlinear-in-the-Parameters Model

In this section we demonstrate the estimation of the nonlinear model in equation (10.2), the data for which are contained in the EViews workfile *nonlin.wf1*. There are no special commands or estimation options required to estimate equation (10.2) since EViews automatically recognizes nonlinearities in the parameters. However, we will no longer be able to simply specify our equation implicitly using the list method in the equation specification dialog box. Instead, we specify the equation by formula, entering the equation explicitly.   Select **Quick/Estimate Equation** and in the equation specification dialog box type:

Y = C(1)*X1 + C(1)^2*X2

We note that '^' is EViews notation for exponentiation. Note also that our EViews output presented below states "Convergence achieved after 1 iterations". This statement indicates that the model has been estimated using a numerical optimization technique rather than the algebraic technique used for models that are linear in the parameters. When estimating models by numerical procedures you will see slight differences in estimates and standard errors from one software package to another. This is because each package uses is own algorithms for these numerical problems.

The best estimate of β from equation (10.2) is 1.1612, which minimizes the sum of squared residuals, Σe_t^2 as illustrated in Figure 10.3. Our results are

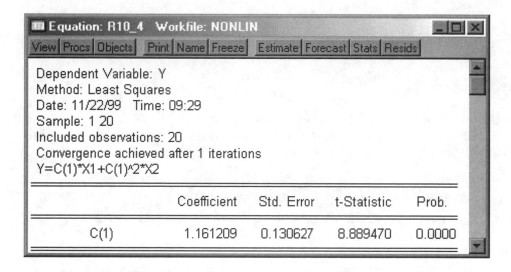

10.3 A Logistic Growth Curve

To replicate the text's estimation of the logistic growth curve for diffusion of technological change in U.S. steel production open the workfile *steel.wf1*, select **Quick/Estimate Equation** and in the equation specification dialog box type

Y = C(1)/(1+EXP(-C(2)-C(3)*T))

Note that EXP( ) is EViews notation for the exponential functional form, e^x. Our results match Table 10.4 in the text.

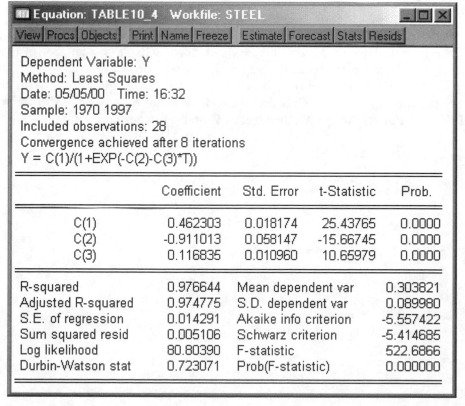

To calculate the year at which the inflection point occurs, type the following command in the EViews command window.

scalar inflect = -c(2)/c(3)

To test the hypothesis that the point of inflection occurs in year 11, 1980, from the equation's toolbar, select **View/Coefficient Tests/Wald - Coefficient Restrictions…**, and enter the restriction -c(2)/c(3) = 11 in the **Wald Test** dialog box. Our results match those found at the bottom of Table 10.4 in the text.

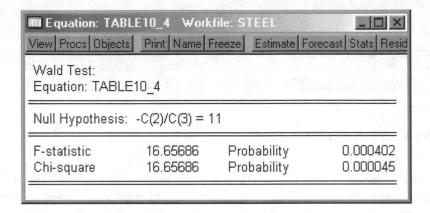

We note that the *p*-values for either the F or Chi-square large sample tests are small enough to allow us to reject the null hypothesis that the inflection point occurred in period 11, 1980.

10.4 Poisson Regression

Here we estimate the text's model of count data for visits to Lake Keepit in Australia. Data on visits (VISITS), distance from Lake Keepit (DIST), household income (INC), and number of household family members (MEMB) are found in the workfile *keepit.wf1*. Open the workfile and select **Quick/Estimate Equation** from the EViews menubar. Though our results will vary slightly from those presented in the text, we will use the built-in EViews estimation method for count data. In the **Equation Specification** dialog box under **Estimation Settings: Method**, select **Count – Integer count data**.

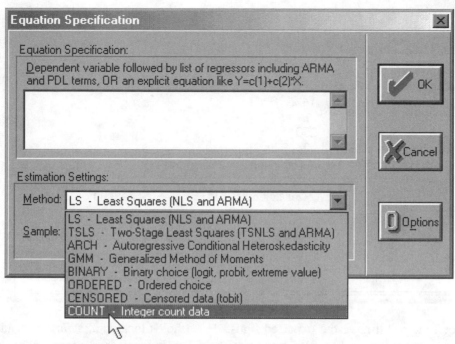

Next, enter the dependent variable, VISITS, followed by the constant, C, and the three independent variables DIST, INC, and MEMB, in list form.

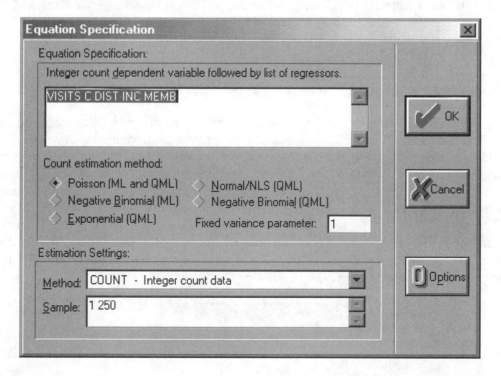

Our results, which closely approximate those in Table 10.6 in the text are presented below

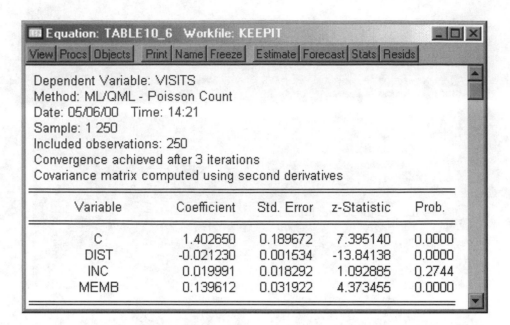

Note that the coefficients all have the expected signs. Households located at a further distance from Lake Keepit make fewer visits annually. Households with higher incomes and more family members make more yearly visits to Lake Keepit. The *p*-values indicate that the constant, C, and the coefficients on DIST and MEMB are statistically significant, while the coefficient on INC is not statistically significant. To calculate the probability that a household located 50 miles from Lake Keepit with an income of $60,000 and three family members visits the lake less than three times per year, enter the following equation based on EViews' built-in Poisson distribution in the EViews command window:

scalar prob3 = @cpoisson(2,@EXP(C(1) + C(2)*50 + C(3)*6 + C(4)*3))

Here we use the EViews built-in cumulative Poisson probability function, @cpoisson, to calculate the probability. This saves us the trouble of calculating the individual probabilities $P(y = 0)$, $P(y = 1)$, and $P(y = 2)$, and then summing them. In this equation, we are calculating the cumulative probability of 2 visits, hence the number 2 is entered as the first argument inside the parentheses for the @cpoisson function. The individual mean, μ_i, is the @EXP( ) expression listed as the second argument inside the parentheses, within which we have entered the specific characteristics for this household, DIST = 50, INC = 6, and MEMB = 3. Note that we use the EViews convention that C(1), C(2), and C(3) refer to the most recent regression model estimated. Had we run another model since the Poisson model, these placeholders in the coefficient vector would contain incorrect values. Our result is: prob3 = 0.567, which is very close to the text estimate of 0.564.

Scalar PROB3 = 0.566908385818

Chapter 11 Heteroskedasticity

11.1 Diagnosing Heteroskedasticity

This chapter introduces the nature, consequences, and detection of heteroskedastic error terms (e_t). To explore the implications of heteroskedasticity, we will employ the workfiles *foodexp.wf1* and *wheat.wf1*. Open the workfile *foodexp.wf1*, click on **Quick/Estimate Equation**, enter the food expenditure equation (11.1.4) in the **Equation Specification** dialog box, and click **OK**. Our results are

```
Equation: EQ11_1_4   Workfile: FOODEXP
View Procs Objects   Print Name Freeze   Estimate Forecast Stats Resids
```

Dependent Variable: Y
Method: Least Squares
Date: 10/27/99   Time: 09:15
Sample: 1 40
Included observations: 40

Variable	Coefficient	Std. Error	t-Statistic	Prob.
C	40.76756	22.13865	1.841465	0.0734
X	0.128289	0.030539	4.200777	0.0002

R-squared	0.317118	Mean dependent var		130.3130
Adjusted R-squared	0.299148	S.D. dependent var		45.15857
S.E. of regression	37.80536	Akaike info criterion		10.15149
Sum squared resid	54311.33	Schwarz criterion		10.23593
Log likelihood	-201.0297	F-statistic		17.64653
Durbin-Watson stat	2.370373	Prob(F-statistic)		0.000155

As an early warning for heteroskedasticity, we visually inspect the residuals by examining a simple scatterplot of the actual data points including the estimated expenditure function. Your text presents this information in Figure 11.1, which we create in EViews with the following steps:

- Holding down the <Ctrl> key, select X and then Y from your workfile
- Note: EViews will plot the first variable selected on the horizontal axis, so always select your "X" variable first.
- Release the <Ctrl> key and double click on either variable
- Select **Open Group**
- Select **View/Graph/Scatter/Scatter with Regression**

Alternatively, you can follow these steps:

- Select **Quick/Graph** from the EViews menubar.
- List the series you want to plot. If you want to create a scatterplot, be sure to list your horizontal axis variable first

- Select **Scatter Diagram** from the Graph Type listbox, and click OK.

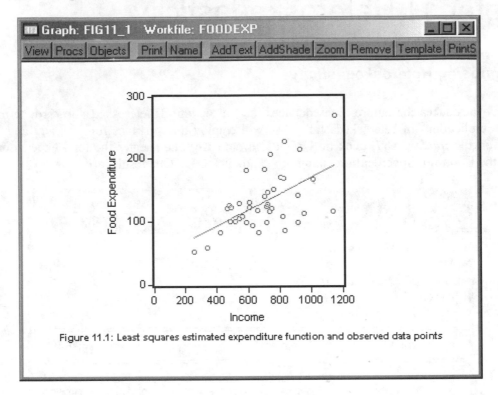

Figure 11.1: Least squares estimated expenditure function and observed data points

Note from Figure 11.1 how the errors increase at higher income levels. This is our first casual empirical evidence of the presence of heteroskedasticity. As noted in *UE/2*, it is quite common to observe heteroskedastic error terms that increase in absolute value with higher incomes. The choice constraints on lower income households suggest that our models will be estimated more precisely for lower incomes than for higher incomes.

11.2 White's Approximate Estimator for the Variance of the Least Squares Estimator

The text indicates that the standard errors of the ordinary least squares coefficient estimates are incorrect. Here we use EViews to obtain White's corrected standard error estimates for the coefficients of our food expenditure model. Select **Quick/Estimate Equation** from the EViews menubar and click on the **Options** button found at the lower right of the Equation Specification dialog box. In the Equation Options dialog box check **Heteroskedasticity Consistent Covariance** and **White**, and then click **OK**.

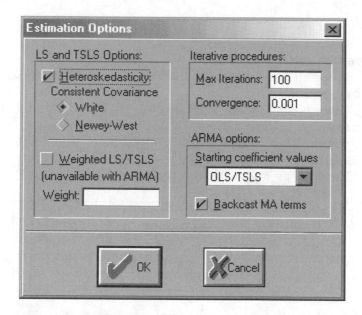

When we return to the Equation Specification dialog box, we must ensure that we have entered the equation **Y C X** and then click **OK**. Our results are

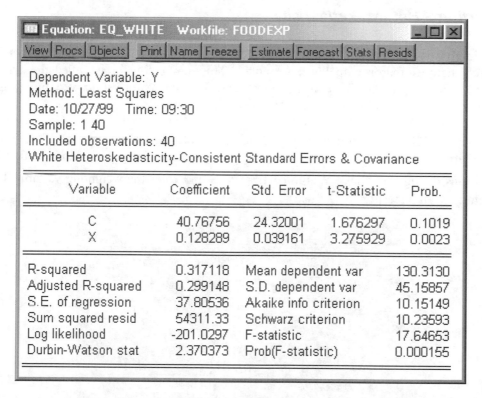

The White standard errors reported by EViews are not the same values as those reported in the text but they are very close approximations. The text results were obtained from a different software package, which accounts for the minor differences.

Next, we compare the confidence intervals from the **Incorrect** model with those from the **White** model by constructing a storage vector for the lower and upper bounds of the respective intervals. To do this, we type the following commands into the EViews command window:

Create a storage vector

coef(4) confid

Incorrect Model: lower bound

confid(1) = eq11_1_4.@coefs(2) - @qtdist(.95,38)*(eq11_1_4.@stderrs(2)

Incorrect Model: upper bound

confid(2) = eq11_1_4.@coefs(2) + @qtdist(.95,38)*(eq11_1_4.@stderrs(2)

White Model: lower bound

confid(3) = eq_white.@coefs(2) - @qtdist(.95,38)*(eq_white.@stderrs(2)

White Model: upper bound

confid(4) = eq_white.@coefs(2) + @qtdist(.95,38)*(eq_white.@stderrs(2)

Model	Estimate
Incorrect Model: Lower Bound	0.076801
Incorrect Model: Upper Bound	0.179776
White Model: Lower Bound	0.062265
White Model: Upper Bound	0.194312

Note: These upper and lower bounds differ from those presented in your text due to rounding procedures.

11.3 Proportional Heteroskedasticity

Rather than simply recalculating the coefficient standard errors according to the White procedure, we now seek an entirely new estimator with lower variance. This new estimator is called the generalized least squares (GLS) estimator. As the text indicates, the GLS estimator is derived by transforming the variables to produce a statistical model with homoskedastic errors.

To reproduce result (R11.4) in the text, select **Quick/Estimate Equation** from the EViews menubar and click on the **Options** button found at the lower right of the Equation Specification dialog box. In the **Equation Options** dialog box check **Weighted LS/TSLS** and enter the weighting variable $1/\sqrt{x}$, which in EViews notation can be written as **X^(-.5)**.

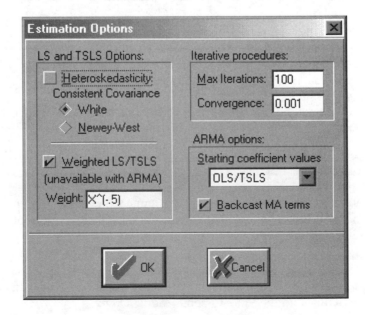

Our results are

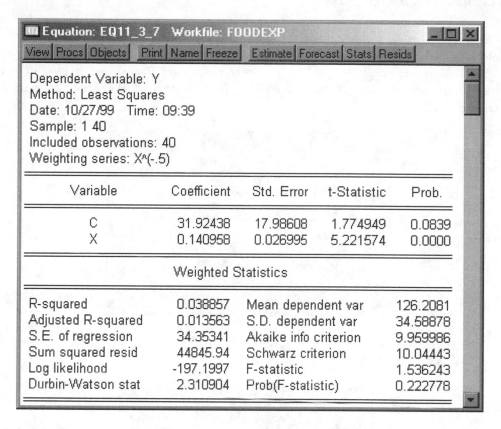

To compare the standard errors from the Incorrect, White, and GLS models in a single table, create a storage vector and fill each element with the relevant standard errors. We illustrate below for the standard errors of the slope coefficient b_2:

Create a storage vector

coef(3) stderrs
Incorrect Model: standard error of b_2
stderrs(1) = eq11_1_4.@ stderrs(2)
White Model: standard error of b_2
stderrs(2) = eq_white.@stderrs(2)
GLS Model: standard error of b_2
stderrs(3) = eq11_3_7.@stderrs(2)

Notice that the GLS standard error is smaller than its White Model counterpart. This is what we would expect since GLS is the least variance, or "best" estimator.

Model	se(b_2)
Incorrect Model	0.030539
White Model	0.039161
GLS Model	0.026995

11.4 The Goldfeld-Quandt Test

The Goldfeld-Quandt test provides us with a statistical test for the presence of heteroskedasticity. To form the Goldfeld-Quandt test for the food expenditure problem, we must first sort the data in descending order according to our income variable X. To do this click on **Procs/Sort Series** from the EViews menubar, enter the income variable X in the **Sort Key** field of the **Sort Workfile Series** dialog box, and check **Descending** for the **Sort Order**.

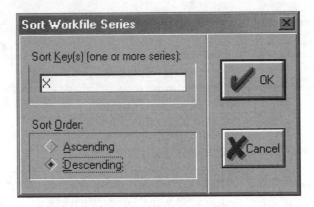

As a check on this process, we select Y and X from our workfile and open a group. We see that the data are now sorted in descending order according to income:

obs	X	Y
1	1154.600	269.0300
2	1141.300	115.4300
3	1014.000	166.2500
4	951.7000	112.8900
5	929.6000	215.4000
6	918.1000	141.0600
7	918.1000	98.70000
8	834.0000	84.94000
9	833.3000	227.1100
10	825.6000	168.9000
11		

Next, we run ordinary least squares on the first 20 observations of the sample and save the standard error of the regression as SIG1. We can use **Quick/Estimate Equation** and name our equation EQ_GQ_01 or we can type the following commands into the EViews command window:

```
SMPL 1 20
EQUATION EQ_GQ_01.LS Y C X
SCALAR SIG1 = @SE
```

> **Note:** Estimating equations is carried out by clicking **Quick/Estimate Equation,** and then filling in the dialog box. Alternatively, the "Equation" command can be entered in the command window. The general form of this command is
>
> Equation *eqname.*LS *dep_var c independent_var*
>
> Where *eqname* is the name of the equation, ".LS" indicates least squares estimation, *dep_var* is the name of the dependent variable, *c* is present if we want to include an intercept, and *independent_var* is a list of explanatory variables. Either approach can be used. More explanation of the EViews command "Equation" is available in EViews Help.

For the last 20 observations we run the regression

```
SMPL 21 40
EQUATION EQ_GQ_02.LS Y C X
SCALAR SIG2 = @SE
```

To create the Goldfeld-Quandt statistic for the food expenditure problem, create a storage vector and fill its cells with the elements of the test using the following EViews commands:

```
COEF(2) GQ                        Creates a storage vector for the test results
GQ(1) = (SIG1^2)/(SIG2^2)         Puts the G-Q F-statistic in cell 1
GQ(2) = @QFDIST(.95,18,18)        Puts the F critical value in cell 2
```

Our results are

Goldfeld-Quandt F Statistic	3.349581
$F_{(.05,18,18)}$ critical value	2.217197

Since the GQ F-statistic 3.35 is greater than the F critical value 2.22, we reject the null hypothesis of no heteroskedasticity, suggesting that the error variance depends on income.

11.5 A Sample with a Heteroskedastic Partition

In this section, we present a model of the supply function for Australian wheat. What makes this model interesting is the presence of a technological improvement – a new variety of wheat introduced after the thirteenth year that is less likely to be damaged by adverse weather conditions. Since we have no explicit weather variable in our sample, weather effects are picked up by the error term, making it quite likely that the introduction of the new strain of wheat will produce heteroskedastic error terms. Open the workfile *wheat.wf1* and select **Quick/Estimate Equation** from the EViews menubar. Type in the model **Q C P T** and change the sample to **1 13**, the first subperiod before the new wheat varieties were introduced. Alternatively, you can type the following commands into the EViews command window:

```
SMPL 1 13
EQUATION EQ01.LS Q C P T
```

Note that we have named this first partition equation EQ01. You will have to perform this task by clicking on the equation's toolbar and entering **EQ01.** This is one of the advantages of using the EQUATION statement above in the EViews command window, as the equation is named and estimated simultaneously with a single command. Repeat this procedure for the second subperiod (observations 14-26) after the new wheat varieties were introduced by using **Quick/Estimate Equation,** changing the sample period to the range pair **14 26**, and naming your equation **EQ02,** or by typing the following commands:

```
SMPL 14 26
EQUATION EQ02.LS Q C P T
```

We will impose homoskedasticity by dividing the model variables by the standard error of the regression from EQ01 for observations 1-13 in the first partition, and by the standard error of the regression from EQ02 for observations 14-26 in the second partition. To transform the variables as found in equation (11.5.5) in your text, using the EViews command window, set your sample to the first partition (observations 1-13) and transform your Y, P, and T variables to Y*, P*, and T* as follows:

SMPL 1 13	**Changes the sample to the first partition**
SCALAR SIG1 = EQ01.@SE	**Creates σ_1 - the std. error from equation 1**
GENR QSTAR = Q/SIG1	**Transforms the dependent variable to q/σ_1**
GENR CSTAR = 1/SIG1	**Transforms the intercept variable to $1/\sigma_1$**
GENR PSTAR = P/SIG1	**Transforms the price variable to p/σ_1**
GENR TSTAR = T/SIG1	**Transforms the time trend variable to t/σ_1**

Next, change your sample to the second partition and transform your variables again with the following EViews commands

SMPL 14 26	**Changes the sample to the second partition**
SCALAR SIG2 = EQ02.@SE	**Creates σ_2 - the std. error from equation 2**
GENR QSTAR = Q/SIG2	**Transforms the dependent variable to q/σ_2**
GENR CSTAR = 1/SIG2	**Transforms the intercept variable to $1/\sigma_2$**
GENR PSTAR = P/SIG2	**Transforms the price variable to p/σ_2**
GENR TSTAR = T/SIG2	**Transforms the time trend variable to t/σ_2**

Note that SIG1 and SIG2 are the square roots of the error variances for Equations 1 and 2 estimated in the workfile and found in equation (R11.7) in your text.

To obtain the estimated equation (R11.8) change to the full sample, SMPL 1 26, click on **Quick/Estimate Equation**, list the transformed variables **QSTAR CSTAR PSTAR TSTAR**, and click **OK**. Be sure to click on the **Name** button on the equation's toolbar and name this equation R11_8.

```
┌─────────────────────────────────────────────────────────────────┐
│ ▦ Equation: R11_8  Workfile: WHEAT                    _ □ ✕       │
│ View│Procs│Objects│ Print│Name│Freeze│ Estimate│Forecast│Stats│Resids│ │
├─────────────────────────────────────────────────────────────────┤
│ Dependent Variable: QSTAR                                         │
│ Method: Least Squares                                             │
│ Date: 10/27/99   Time: 11:05                                      │
│ Sample: 1 26                                                      │
│ Included observations: 26                                         │
```

Variable	Coefficient	Std. Error	t-Statistic	Prob.
CSTAR	138.0541	12.82098	10.76783	0.0000
PSTAR	21.71975	8.923946	2.433873	0.0231
TSTAR	3.283438	0.822638	3.991354	0.0006

R-squared	0.995003	Mean dependent var	21.33577
Adjusted R-squared	0.994568	S.D. dependent var	13.75112
S.E. of regression	1.013481	Akaike info criterion	2.972826
Sum squared resid	23.62431	Schwarz criterion	3.117991
Log likelihood	-35.64674	F-statistic	2289.702
Durbin-Watson stat	1.520419	Prob(F-statistic)	0.000000

Note: EViews produces an estimated standard error of the regression that is close to – but not equal to – one.

Section 11.6 Testing the Variance Assumption

Continuing with the wheat supply example, we plot the residuals from a least squares regression of Q on C, P, and T, ignoring for the moment the heteroskedastic partition. We will refer to this regression as **EQ03**. To reproduce Figure 11.3 in the text, we click on **Quick/Estimate Equation** and list the equation variables **Q C P T**, then click **OK** to run the model on the full sample. Alternatively we could simply type

```
SMPL 1 26
EQUATION EQ03.LS Q C P T
```

Immediately after running the regression, we generate a new series E equal to the residuals:

```
GENR E = RESID
```

To create a scatterplot of the residuals E against time T, choose **Quick/Graph** from the EViews menubar, list the variables **T E**, and click **OK**. Note again that the variable order matters here; EViews plots the first variable on the horizontal axis. When the Graph dialog box opens, choose **Scatter Diagram** from the **Graph Type** dropdown menu and click **OK**. Our EViews graph replicates Figure 11.3 in the text. We can clearly see the heteroskedastic partition from Figure 11.3, as the absolute values of the residuals shrink dramatically after period 13.

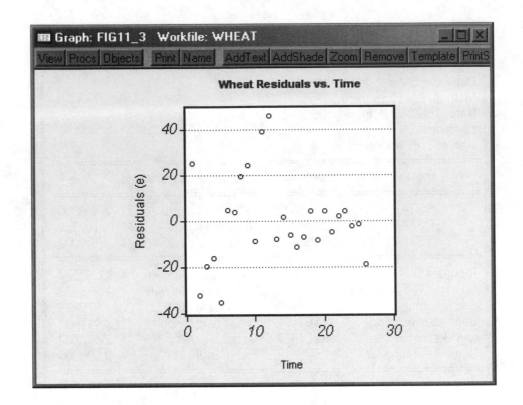

The Goldfeld-Quandt test provides us with a statistical test for the presence of heteroskedasticity. To form the Goldfeld-Quandt test for the wheat supply problem, create a storage vector and fill its cells with the elements of the test using the following EViews commands:

COEF(2) GQ	**Creates a storage vector for the test results**
GQ(1) = (SIG1^2)/(SIG2^2)	**Puts the G-Q F-statistic in cell 1**
GQ(2) = @QFDIST(.95,10,10)	**Puts the F critical value in cell 2**

Our results are

Goldfeld-Quandt F Statistic	11.10902
$F_{(.05,10,10)}$ critical value	2.978237

Since the GQ F-statistic 11.11 is greater than the F critical value 2.98, we reject the null hypothesis of no heteroskedasticity, suggesting that the new wheat strains have lowered the variance in the supply of wheat.

Chapter 12 Autocorrelation

Chapter 12 introduces the violation of assumption 4 of the linear regression model, which states that the random errors (e_t) are uncorrelated. When this assumption is relaxed, we say that the random errors of an ordinary least squares regression model exhibit autocorrelation.

12.1   Residual Plots

To explore the nature, consequences for ordinary least squares estimation, and detection of autocorrelation, open the workfile *sugar.wf1*, click on **Quick/Estimate Equation.** Enter the sugar cane equation LOG(A) C LOG(P) in the **Equation Specification** dialog box, and click **OK**. The results reproduce result R12.1 in the text:

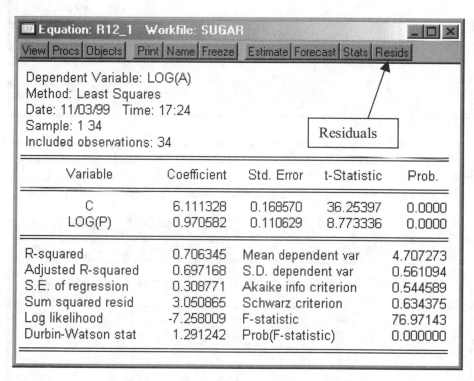

To produce a graph similar to Figure 12.1, click on **Resids** on the equation's toolbar.

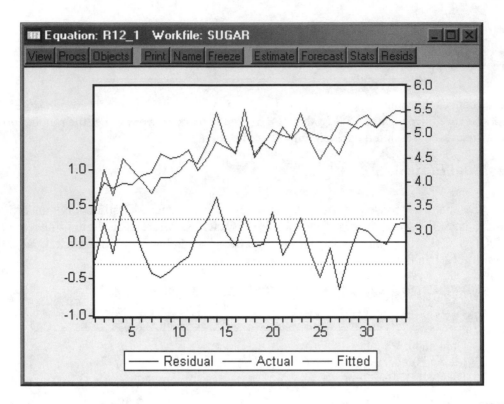

Alternatively, create a trend variable in the command window using the command GENR T = @TREND(1) + 1, and then create a scatterplot of T and RESID by selecting these two variables from the workfile, double-clicking on one of them, and selecting **Open Group**.   Then select **View/Graph/Scatter/Simple Scatter** from the group's toolbar. This reproduces Figure 12.1 in your text:

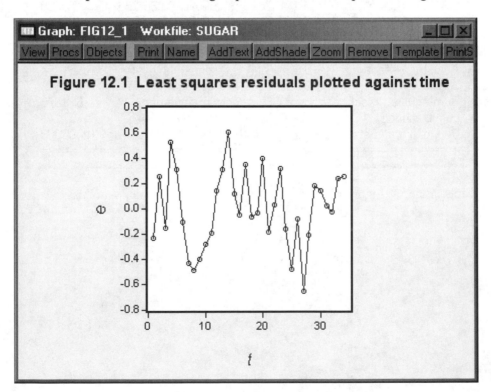

Note the distinct pattern of intertia in the residuals: positive errors follow positive errors and negative errors follow negative errors. This is our first visual evidence of the presence of positive autocorrelation in our model.

EViews will produce other representations of the residuals, which we should explore. One very useful representation is obtained by clicking **View/Actual,Fitted,Residual/Actual,Fitted,Residual Table** in the Equation window.

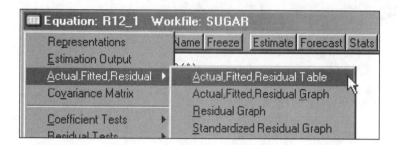

The resulting table and graph sometimes simplifies identifying runs of positive and negative residuals. For example, residuals 6-11 are negative, followed by 12-15 which are positive.

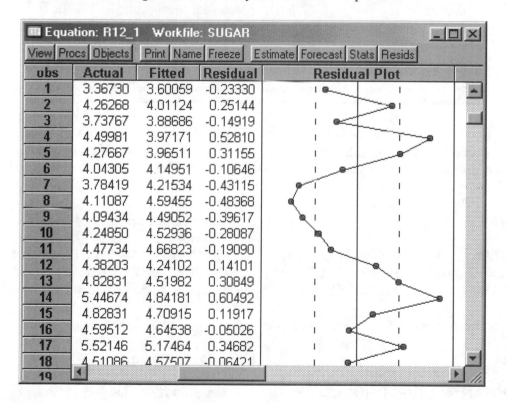

12.2 Implementing Generalized Least Squares

To obtain an estimate of ρ, the first-order autocorrelation coefficient, we save the residuals e_t from result (R12.1) and use them to estimate equation (12.5.4) in the text. To do this, we enter the following commands in the EViews command window:

GENR E = RESID

EQUATION EQ12_5_4.LS E E(-1)

Observe that equation (12.5.4) does not include an intercept.

Our results are

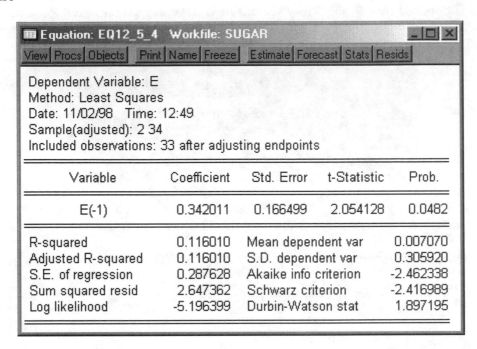

The coefficient on the lagged residuals is our estimate of ρ, $\hat{\rho} = 0.342$. Armed with this estimate we are now ready to conduct the variable transformations shown in equation (12.4.12) in preparation for estimating the generalized least squares (GLS) model of section 12.5. To transform the first observation, enter the following commands in the EViews command window:

SCALAR RHO = C(1)	**Saves our estimate of** ρ
SMPL 1 1	**Changes sample to 1st obs.**
GENR YSTAR = ((1 – RHO^2)^.5)*LOG(A)	**Creates YSTAR from Eq (12.4.11b)**
GENR X2STAR = ((1 – RHO^2)^.5)*LOG(P)	**Creates X2STAR from Eq (12.4.11b)**
GENR X1STAR = ((1 – RHO^2)^.5)	**Creates X1STAR from Eq (12.4.11b)**

To transform observations 2-34, enter the following commands in the EViews command window:

SMPL 2 34	**Changes sample**
GENR YSTAR = LOG(A)-RHO*(LOG(A(-1)))	**Creates YSTAR – Eq (12.4.7a)**
GENR X2STAR = LOG(P)-RHO*(LOG(P(-1)))	**Creates X2STAR – Eq (12.4.7b)**
GENR X1STAR = 1-RHO	**Creates X1STAR – Eq (12.4.7c)**

Note that this transformation produces Table 12.3 of your text.

```
Group: TABLE12_3   Workfile: SUGAR                          _ □ ✕
View Procs Objects   Print Name Freeze   Edit+/- Smpl+/- InsDel Transpose Title Sample
```

obs	X1STAR	LOG(P)	X2STAR	LOG(A)	YSTAR
1	0.939696	-2.586833	-2.430837	3.367296	3.164235
2	0.657989	-2.163745	-1.279021	4.262680	3.111029
3	0.657989	-2.291892	-1.551869	3.737670	2.279788
4	0.657989	-2.204470	-1.420618	4.499810	3.221487
5					

Next we apply generalized least squares to these transformed variables. To obtain result (R12.7), type the following commands in the EViews command window:

SMPL 1 34
EQUATION R12_7.LS YSTAR X1STAR X2STAR

```
Equation: R12_7   Workfile: SUGAR                          _ □ ✕
View Procs Objects   Print Name Freeze   Estimate Forecast Stats Resids
```

Dependent Variable: YSTAR
Method: Least Squares
Date: 11/03/99   Time: 16:30
Sample: 1 34
Included observations: 34

Variable	Coefficient	Std. Error	t-Statistic	Prob.
X1STAR	6.164129	0.212808	28.96575	0.0000
X2STAR	1.006595	0.136930	7.351185	0.0000

R-squared	0.517155	Mean dependent var		3.146282
Adjusted R-squared	0.502066	S.D. dependent var		0.410850
S.E. of regression	0.289914	Akaike info criterion		0.418559
Sum squared resid	2.689608	Schwarz criterion		0.508345
Log likelihood	-5.115503	F-statistic		34.27389
Durbin-Watson stat	1.966447	Prob(F-statistic)		0.000002

12.3   Using EViews for Estimation with AR(1) Errors

In econometrics there are many different ways to do a task which are equivalent in large samples. Software packages choose different methods according to how it fits in with the rest of the package. EViews uses an iterative nonlinear procedure for estimating our GLS model in the presence of autocorrelation. Since the estimation procedure is nonlinear, you will see the note "Convergence achieved after n iterations" just above the coefficient table in your estimation output. The GLS estimates may be obtained by simply appending the term AR(1), which stands for autoregressive first-order, to the end of the equation specification list:

EQUATION R12_7AR1.LS LOG(A) C LOG(P) AR(1)

Our results are

```
Equation: R12_7_AR1   Workfile: SUGAR                 _ □ ×
View Procs Objects   Print Name Freeze   Estimate Forecast Stats Resids

Dependent Variable: LOG(A)
Method: Least Squares
Date: 11/03/99   Time: 15:04
Sample(adjusted): 2 34
Included observations: 33 after adjusting endpoints
Convergence achieved after 4 iterations

     Variable      Coefficient   Std. Error   t-Statistic    Prob.

        C           6.089203     0.239990    25.37273     0.0000
      LOG(P)        0.944013     0.163416     5.776759     0.0000
      AR(1)         0.339161     0.172029     1.971530     0.0579

R-squared           0.690616    Mean dependent var    4.747879
Adjusted R-squared  0.669990    S.D. dependent var    0.516579
S.E. of regression  0.296757    Akaike info criterion 0.494700
Sum squared resid   2.641936    Schwarz criterion     0.630746
Log likelihood     -5.162545    F-statistic          33.48339
Durbin-Watson stat  1.899647    Prob(F-statistic)     0.000000

Inverted AR Roots        .34
```

These estimates differ slightly from those presented in the text due to the different technique employed by EViews and the treatment of the first observation. Note however that the EViews estimate of $\rho = 0.339$ is a close approximation to the estimate we obtained in equation (12.5.4), $\rho = 0.342$

12.4   The Durbin-Watson Test for Autocorrelation

As *UE/2* indicates, often we need a more sophisticated technique than visual inspection to discern the presence of autocorrelation. Most software packages – and EViews is no exception – automatically produce a statistic called the Durbin-Watson after each regression. It is found at the bottom left-hand corner of the EViews output. The Durbin-Watson (d) statistic is approximately functionally related to the autocorrelation coefficient ρ as follows: $d = 2(1 - \rho)$. When $d = 2$, $\rho = 0$, that is, there is no evidence of autocorrelation in the model. Hence, researchers generally apply a rule of thumb, comparing the Durbin-Watson (d) statistic to 2 to determine the presence of autocorrelation. If $d < 2$ there is evidence of positive autocorrelation; if $d = 0$, which implies $\rho = 1$, there is evidence of perfect positive autocorrelation.

We reproduce below result (R12.1) in EViews:

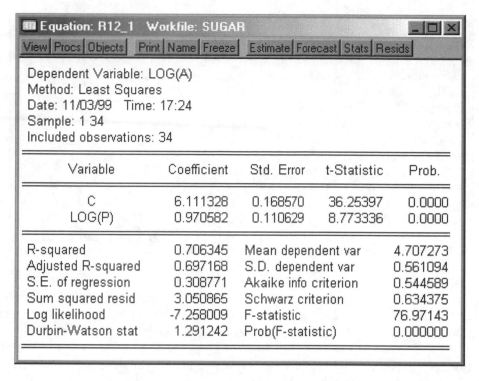

Our Durbin-Watson statistic is $d = 1.291$, which is considerably less than 2 and likely indicates the presence of positive autocorrelation in our model. Note that the first-order autocorrelation coefficient implied by this Durbin-Watson is $\hat{\rho} \cong 1 - d/2 = 1 - 1.291/2 = 0.355$, which is slightly higher than our previous estimates. EViews does not provide the p-value of the Durbin-Watson test. Tables of critical values for the Durbin-Watson statistic are found in Table 5 in *UE/2*.

12.5   The Lagrange Multiplier Test for Autocorrelation

The Lagrange Multiplier test is easily conducted in EViews. We enter the following commands in the EViews command window

```
GENR E1 = E(-1)                      Creates the lagged residual series e(-1)
SMPL 1 1                             Sets the sample to the first observation
GENR E1 = 0                          Sets e(0) to zero
SMPL 1 34                            Returns to the full sample
EQUATION R12_9.LS LOG(A) C LOG(P) E1  Estimates equation (12.6.8)
```

Our results are

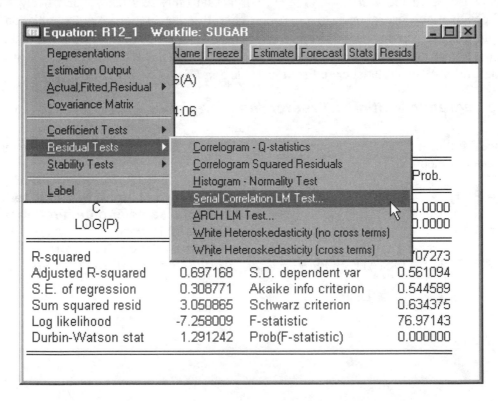

We have highlighted the *t*-statistic and its associated *p*-value for the coefficient on E1, the lagged residuals (e_{t-1}) from the original equation. The *F*-statistic, 4.022, reported in result (R12.9) in the text is simply the square of the *t*-statistic, 2.006. Since the *p*-value, 0.054 is greater than our significance level of 5%, the Lagrange Multiplier test fails to reject the null hypothesis of no autocorrelation.

This simple test is automated by EViews. In the EViews equation window **R12_1**, click on **View/Residual Tests/Serial Correlation LM Test**.

In the dialog box that opens enter 1, indicating the number of lagged residuals to include:

The result is

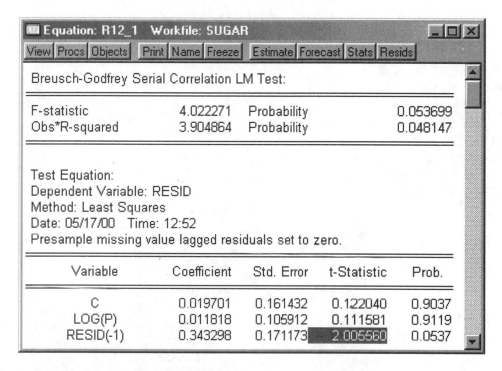

These results agree with those in result R12.9.

12.6   Prediction with AR(1) Errors

As the text indicates, an improvement in prediction can be made in the presence of AR(1) error terms. The improvement is due to the systematic correlation between errors in successive periods as represented by the third term on the right-hand-side of equation (12.7.5). To predict the logarithm of sugar cane area planted for periods 35 and 36, enter the following commands into the EViews command window:

```
EQUATION  R12_7.LS YSTAR X1STAR X2STAR
SCALAR LNA34 = LOG(A(@DTOO("34")))
SCALAR LNP34 = LOG(P(@DTOO("34")))
SCALAR E34 = LNA34 - C(1) - C(2)*LNP34
SCALAR Y35 = C(1) + C(2)*LOG(.4) + RHO*E34
SCALAR Y36 = C(1) + C(2)*LOG(.4) + (RHO^2)*E34
```

Re-estimates R12.7
Calculates ln(A_T)
Calculates ln(P_T)
Calculates e_T
Calculates Y_{T+1}
Calculates Y_{T+2}

where E34 is the final period error term e_T in equation (12.7.6) and we have re-estimated equation (12.5.7) without change simply to ensure that the coefficient vector C is the correct one to use for this problem. Alternatively, we could replace each of the C(n) above with EQ12_5_7.@COEFS(n), which is somewhat cumbersome for long equation names. Note we have used the EViews command **@DTOO(·)** to extract the values of the 34th observations for area (A) and price (P) from the sample. DTOO stands for "date-to-observation" and is a very handy tool for assigning a particular observation value of a series to a scalar for further calculations. The values Y35 and Y36 are the predicted logarithms of the area planted in periods 35 and 36. To obtain the predicted values in acres type

SCALAR Y35_ACRES = EXP(Y35)   **Calculates Y_{T+1} in acres**
SCALAR Y36_ACRES = EXP(Y36)   **Calculates Y_{T+2} in acres**

To place the relevant values from this prediction in a table, enter the following commands in the EViews command window, and then freeze the output as TABLE12_7. Note: This table is not found in the text.

COEF(7) PREDICT
PREDICT(1) = LNA34
PREDICT(2) = LNP34
PREDICT(3) = E34
PREDICT(4) = Y35
PREDICT(5) = Y36
PREDICT(6) = Y35_ACRES
PREDICT(7) = Y36_ACRES

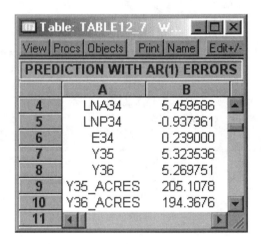

12.7   Using EViews for Prediction with AR(1) Errors

To use EViews prediction tools, we must first change the **workfile range**. On the workfile toolbar, click **Procs/Change workfile Range**

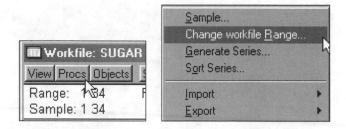

In the resulting dialog box increase the number of observations to 36.

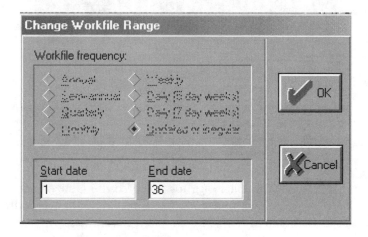

- Open the spreadsheet view of the series *P*, click on the toolbar button **Edit+/-**.
- Scroll to observations 35 and 36, entering .4 for each, representing the sugar cane price in each of the new periods.
- Click the toolbar button **Edit+/-** again, and then close the spreadsheet.

To use the EViews Forecast capabilities we must re-estimate the GLS model using EViews.

- Double-click on equation-object r12_7_ar1.
- On the equation tool bar, click on **Estimate** and then OK, which places the equation estimates in memory again.
- Click on **Forecast** in the equation window

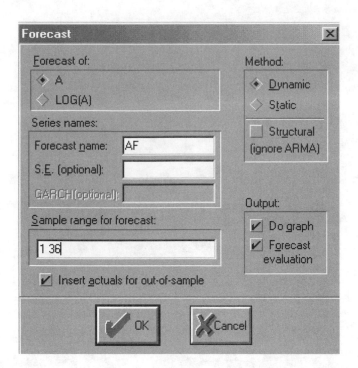

In the resulting dialog box specify the sample range for the forecast. Note choices that we can make, such as, choosing a forecast of A or LOG(A), and choosing a method called Dynamic or Static. Further details of these methods are available in EViews Help, under **Forecasting**.

> **Note:** EViews uses forecasting techniques that account for autocorrelation, as we have in section 12.6. However, econometrics packages, including EViews, use more general techniques than we have, so they can deal with other forms of autocorrelation with the click of a button. The procedures they use will not produce the same forecasts that we have obtained. The method we have shown in section 12.6 is "best" for the AR(1) model. It is tempting to use built-in features of software programs because it is so easy. Before you do, however, check it out, either in the documentation for the program, or with an econometrician.

Chapter 13 Random Regressors and Moment Based Estimation

Chapter 13 introduces the violation of assumption 4 of the linear regression model, which states that the regressors (x_{it}) are nonrandom. When this assumption is relaxed, we say that the random errors of an ordinary least squares regression model exhibit autocorrelation. To begin our consideration of estimation in the simple linear regression framework in the presence of random regressors, we open the workfile *table13-1.wf1*.

13.1 The Inconsistency of the Least Squares Estimator When cov(x,e) ≠ 0

To reproduce Figure 13.1, showing the positive correlation between the x and e generated by the Monte Carlo experiment discussed in the text, we select X and E from the workfile, double-click on one of the series, and select **Open Group**. We then change the view to a simple scatterplot by clicking on **View/Graph/Scatter/Simple Scatter**. The resulting view is saved as a graph object named FIG13_1 in the workfile and appears below.

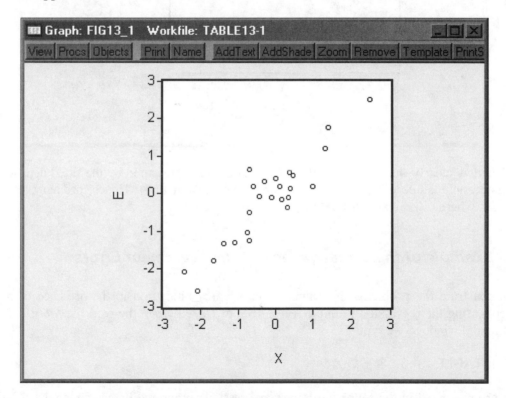

To generate Figure 13.2, select X, Y, YHAT, and EY from the workfile, double-click on one of these variables, and select **Open Group**. After the group is open as a spreadsheet, select **View/Graph/Scatter/Simple Scatter**, double-click on the main graph area, and check **Regression line** under **Scatter Diagram** in the lower right-hand corner of the **Graph Options** dialog box.

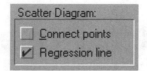

The resulting graph replicates Figure 13.2 in the text as shown below.

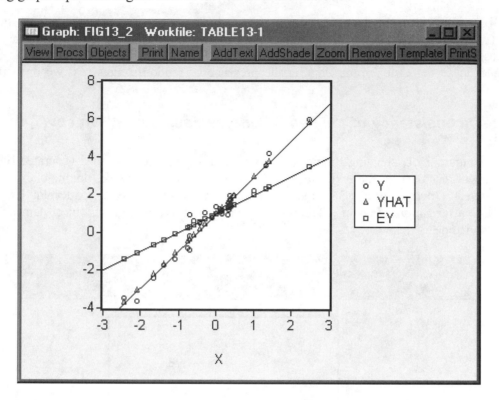

Figure 13.2 shows clearly that the slope of the regression line represented by the fitted dependent variable YHAT overstates the slope of the true population regression function. Hence, ordinary least squares is invalid in cases where x and e are correlated.

13.2   An Example of the Consequences of Measurement Errors

Here we demonstrate the problems of ordinary least squares estimation in the presence of measurement errors by replicating the regression found in Table 13.3 of *UE/2*. Open the workfile *table13-2.wf1*. In the EViews command window, we type

EQUATION TABLE13_3.LS Y C X

Our results are presented in the following EViews regression output and its accompanying ANOVA table, which we generated using the *anova* program we first introduced in chapter 6. See chapter 6 for instructions on how to apply *anova* to the latest regression equation.

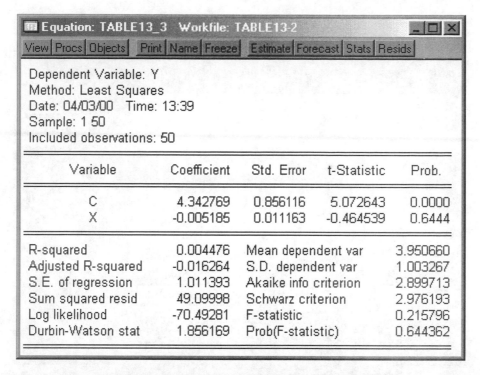

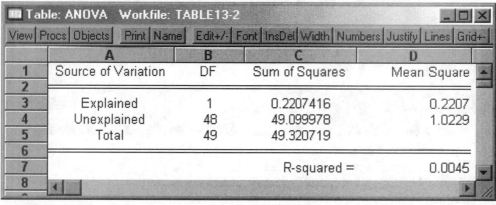

Note that the sign of the coefficient on income (X), is negative, implying a negative marginal propensity to save which is contrary to economic theory. Applying ordinary least squares in the presence of measurement error often produces such counter-theoretical regression results.

13.3 An Empirical Example of Instrumental Variables Estimation

We now turn our attention to the method of instrumental variables estimation described in the text. Instrumental variables estimation produces consistent estimators in the presence of correlation between a random regressor, *x*, and the error term, *e*. To obtain the instrumental variables estimates of the savings function presented in Table 13.4 in the text, we select **Quick/Estimate Equation**, and in the **Equation Specification** dialog box under **Estimation Settings**, change the **Method** to: **TSLS – Two-Stage Least Squares (TSNLS and ARMA)**. Next we enter the savings equation in list form **Y C X**, in the **Equation Specification** field. Finally, we list the instrument, Z, in the **Instrument List** field.

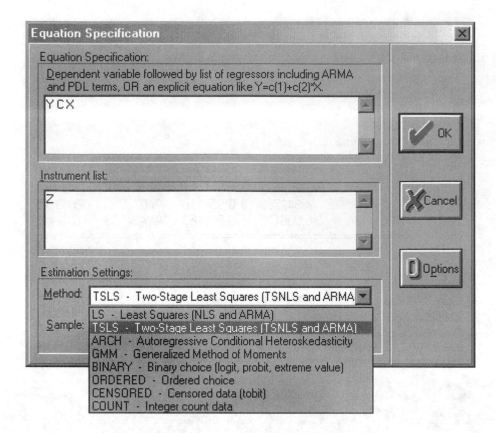

Our results replicate Table 13.4 in *UE/2*:

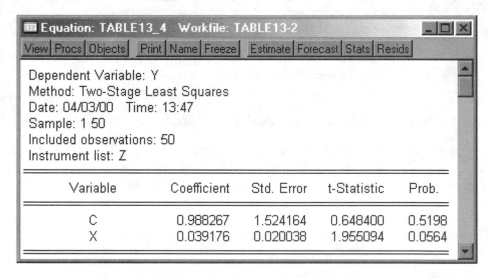

Note that under instrumental variables estimation our estimated marginal propensity to save, the coefficient on income (X) now has the theoretically correct positive sign, is of plausible magnitude, 0.039, and is statistically significant under a one-tailed test. All of these results represent a vast improvement over the ordinary least squares results we obtained in Table 13.3.

13.4   An Empirical Example of the Hausman Test

Here we conduct the Hausman Test for correlation between an explanatory variable, x, and the error term. We continue with the savings example and test for correlation between income (X) and the error term, e. We enter the following commands in the EViews command window:

EQUATION HAUSMAN.LS X C Z   **Estimates the step 1 regression**
GENR VHAT = RESID   **Saves the residuals from step 1 as VHAT**
EQUATION TABLE13_5.LS Y C X VHAT   **Estimates the artificial regression**

Our results are

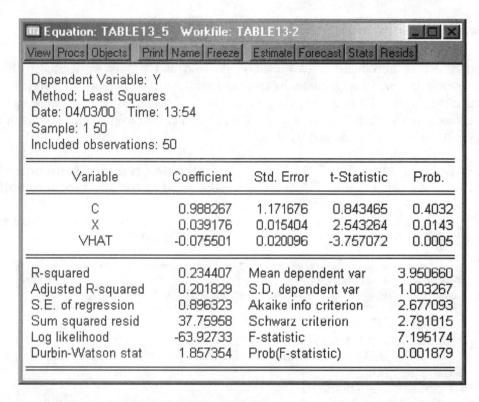

Note that the t-statistic for the coefficient on the residuals from the step one regression is -3.757. The p-value of this test clearly shows that the t-statistic is statistically significant at the 1% level, so we reject the null hypothesis of no correlation between income (X) and the error term e in favor of the alternative that x and e are correlated.

Note: If you forget how to carry out the Hausman test, use EViews Help. An illustration is given that is similar to the one above

Chapter 14 Simultaneous Equations Models

Until now, we have considered estimation and hypothesis testing in a variety of single equation models. Here we introduce models for the joint estimation of two or more equations. While there are countless applications for simultaneous equations models in economics, some applications with which you will be familiar include market demand and supply models and the multi-equation Keynesian models that we analyze in macroeconomics.

14.1 Estimating the Reduced Form

In this section, the text introduces a two-equation demand and supply model for truffles, a French gourmet mushroom delicacy. To estimate the truffles model in EViews, open the workfile *truffles.wf1*. We first estimate the reduced form equations of section 14.7.2 by regressing each endogenous variable, q, and p, on the exogenous variables, *ps, di,* and *pf*. We can quickly accomplish this task with the following statements typed in the EViews command window:

EQUATION TABLE14_2A.LS Q C PS DI PF   **Estimates reduced form equation for q**
EQUATION TABLE14_2B.LS P C PS DI PF   **Estimates reduced form equation for p**

The results of these two commands are shown as Tables 14.2a and 14.2b below. Note that these are simply tabular views of the EViews equation objects of the same name.

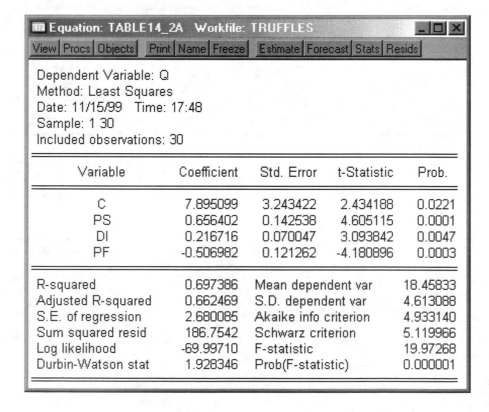

EViews equation window: Equation: TABLE14_2A Workfile: TRUFFLES

Dependent Variable: Q
Method: Least Squares
Date: 11/15/99   Time: 17:48
Sample: 1 30
Included observations: 30

Variable	Coefficient	Std. Error	t-Statistic	Prob.
C	7.895099	3.243422	2.434188	0.0221
PS	0.656402	0.142538	4.605115	0.0001
DI	0.216716	0.070047	3.093842	0.0047
PF	-0.506982	0.121262	-4.180896	0.0003

R-squared	0.697386	Mean dependent var	18.45833
Adjusted R-squared	0.662469	S.D. dependent var	4.613088
S.E. of regression	2.680085	Akaike info criterion	4.933140
Sum squared resid	186.7542	Schwarz criterion	5.119966
Log likelihood	-69.99710	F-statistic	19.97268
Durbin-Watson stat	1.928346	Prob(F-statistic)	0.000001

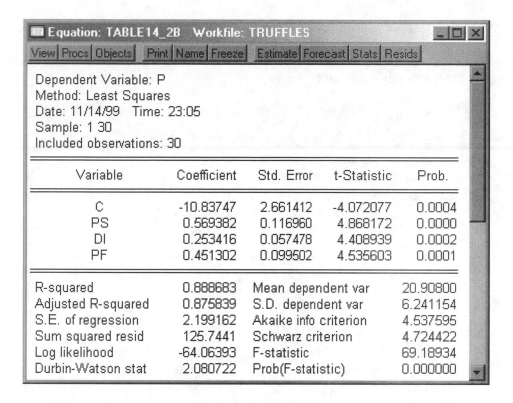

14.2 Two-Stage Least Squares Estimation of an Equation

Any identified equation within a system of simultaneous can be estimated by two-stage least squares (*2sls*). Click on **Quick/Estimate Equation**.

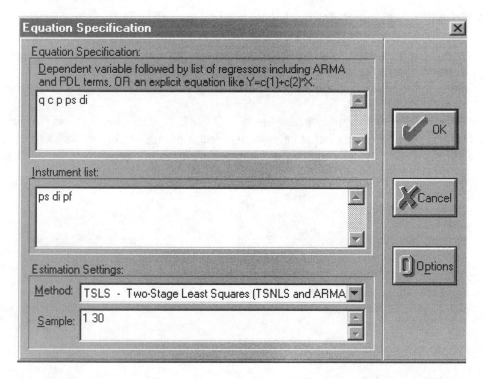

To estimate the demand equation by *2sls* select the method to be TSLS, and fill in the demand equation variables in **Equation specification,** the upper area of the dialog box, and list all the exogenous variables in the system in the **Instrument list**. Click **OK**. Name the resulting equation **demand**. Repeat the same procedure to estimate the supply equation by *2sls*.

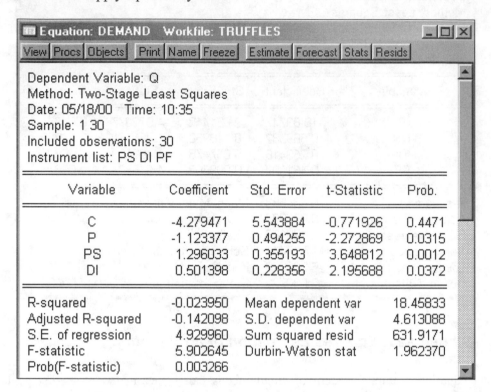

14.3   Two-Stage Least Squares Estimation of a System of Equations

As noted in section 14.2 we can apply *2sls* equation by equation for all the identified equations within a system of equations. If all the equations in the system are identified, then all the equations can be estimated in one step.

We introduce a new EViews object here: the SYSTEM. From the EViews menubar, click on **Objects/New Object**, select **System**, name the system object **TABLE14_3**, and click **OK**.

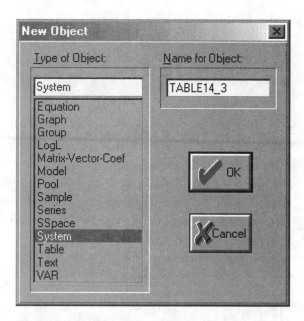

Next, enter the system equation specification given in equations (14.7.1) and (14.7.2). Note that you must enter a line that contains the exogenous (determined outside the model) variables in the system, *ps*, *di*, and *pf*. In the context of two-stage least squares estimation of our truffles system, EViews refers to these exogenous variables as "instruments". Enter the line **INST PS DI PF** directly below the supply equation, and click **Estimate** on the system's toolbar.

To reproduce the results found in Tables 14.3a and 14.3b in your text, under **Estimation Method**, check the **Two-Stage Least Squares** checkbox, and click **OK**.

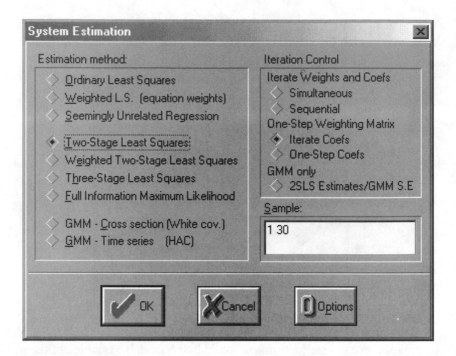

Our results replicate Table 14.3 in the text. **Note:** The output is truncated in this view and only includes estimation details for the demand curve. Use the scrollbar on the right side of this system object to scroll down and view the estimation results for the supply curve. EViews reports the estimated coefficients from all of the equations in the system together at the top of the output and then provides a convenient representation of each equation estimated below the estimation results. For example, from the estimation output we see that the demand curve is

Equation: Q=C(1)+C(2)*P+C(3)*PS+C(4)*DI
Observations: 30

The equation reference provides us with a clear reminder that for interpreting the demand equation, C(1) is the intercept and C(2), C(3), and C(4) are the coefficients on truffle price (P), price of substitutes (PS), and disposable income (DI), respectively. This feature is particularly helpful when we are dealing with systems of many equations and many coefficients.

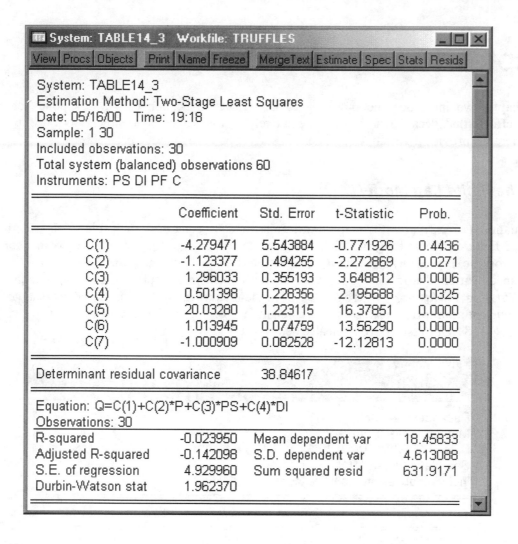

System: TABLE14_3
Estimation Method: Two-Stage Least Squares
Date: 05/16/00   Time: 19:18
Sample: 1 30
Included observations: 30
Total system (balanced) observations 60
Instruments: PS DI PF C

	Coefficient	Std. Error	t-Statistic	Prob.
C(1)	-4.279471	5.543884	-0.771926	0.4436
C(2)	-1.123377	0.494255	-2.272869	0.0271
C(3)	1.296033	0.355193	3.648812	0.0006
C(4)	0.501398	0.228356	2.195688	0.0325
C(5)	20.03280	1.223115	16.37851	0.0000
C(6)	1.013945	0.074759	13.56290	0.0000
C(7)	-1.000909	0.082528	-12.12813	0.0000

Determinant residual covariance	38.84617

Equation: Q=C(1)+C(2)*P+C(3)*PS+C(4)*DI
Observations: 30

R-squared	-0.023950	Mean dependent var	18.45833
Adjusted R-squared	-0.142098	S.D. dependent var	4.613088
S.E. of regression	4.929960	Sum squared resid	631.9171
Durbin-Watson stat	1.962370		

Chapter 15 Distributed Lag Models

In this chapter we introduce the modeling of lag effects in economics. Many policy changes have economic effects that decay over time. Alternatively, perhaps the economic effects first build and then die out. Here we provide a variety of solutions to such dynamic economic problems.

15.1   The Finite Lag Model

Using equation (15.2.2) and the capital expenditure data contained in Table 15.1, we illustrate an unrestricted finite distributed lag model with lag length $n = 8$. To replicate the results in Table 15.2, we open the workfile *capexp.wf1*, select **Quick/Estimate Equation** and type **Y C X(0 TO -8)** in the equation specification dialog box. Note the EViews method for specifying multiple adjacent lags is *var_name(firstlag TO lastlag)*, where *lastlag* $\leq n$, the maximum lag length. In the present case, we want to include current appropriations x_0, as well as eight lags of appropriations, so *var_name* = X, *firstlag* = 0, and *lastlag* = -8. Our results are presented below

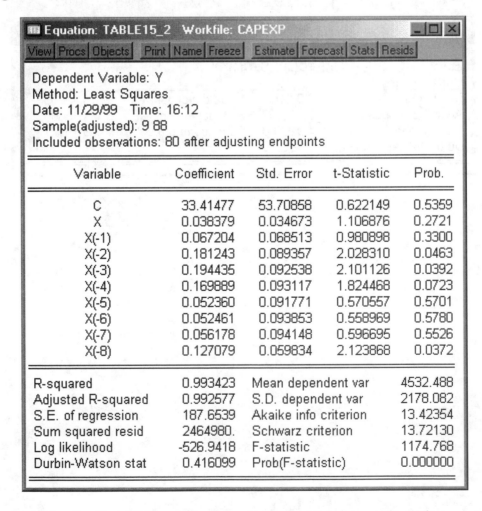

Equation: TABLE15_2   Workfile: CAPEXP

View | Procs | Objects | Print | Name | Freeze | Estimate | Forecast | Stats | Resids

Dependent Variable: Y
Method: Least Squares
Date: 11/29/99   Time: 16:12
Sample(adjusted): 9 88
Included observations: 80 after adjusting endpoints

Variable	Coefficient	Std. Error	t-Statistic	Prob.
C	33.41477	53.70858	0.622149	0.5359
X	0.038379	0.034673	1.106876	0.2721
X(-1)	0.067204	0.068513	0.980898	0.3300
X(-2)	0.181243	0.089357	2.028310	0.0463
X(-3)	0.194435	0.092538	2.101126	0.0392
X(-4)	0.169889	0.093117	1.824468	0.0723
X(-5)	0.052360	0.091771	0.570557	0.5701
X(-6)	0.052461	0.093853	0.558969	0.5780
X(-7)	0.056178	0.094148	0.596695	0.5526
X(-8)	0.127079	0.059834	2.123868	0.0372

R-squared	0.993423	Mean dependent var	4532.488
Adjusted R-squared	0.992577	S.D. dependent var	2178.082
S.E. of regression	187.6539	Akaike info criterion	13.42354
Sum squared resid	2464980.	Schwarz criterion	13.72130
Log likelihood	-526.9418	F-statistic	1174.768
Durbin-Watson stat	0.416099	Prob(F-statistic)	0.000000

To obtain a plot of the distributed lag weights (β_i) as in Figure 15.4, we use the EViews program **_URLAG_** available for download from the textbook website, ***http://www.wiley.com/college/hill***. This program will plot the first eight lag weights from the most recently estimated unrestricted distributed lag equation. Open the program, click on **Run**, and then click **OK**

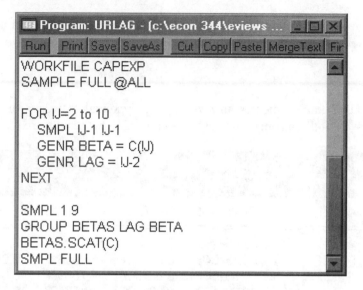

After freezing the group as a graph named **fig15_3** and adding titles we have the following replication of Figure 15.3 in the text.

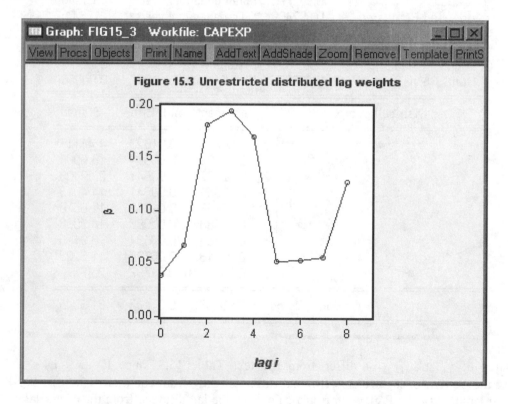

15.2   Polynomial Distributed Lags

To estimate the polynomial distributed lag (PDL) model of equation (15.2.7) and reproduce the results of Tables 15.3 and 15.4, select **Quick/Estimate Equation** and enter the following equation in list form:

Y C PDL(X,8,2)

In EViews notation, PDL(X,*n*,*q*) indicates an *q-th* order polynomial of *n* lags of the variable X. In the present application, X = capital appropriations, *n* = 8 and *q* = 2. Our results are

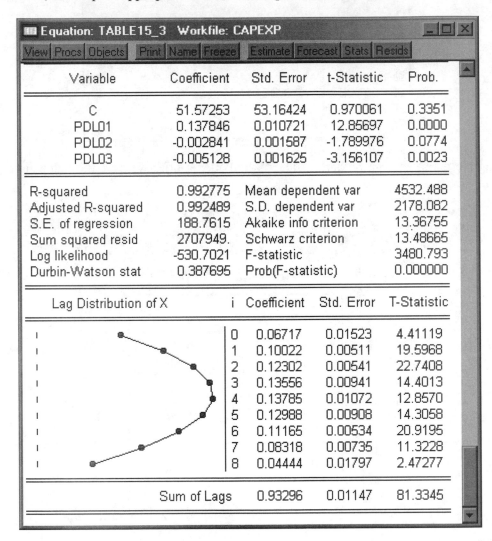

Variable	Coefficient	Std. Error	t-Statistic	Prob.
C	51.57253	53.16424	0.970061	0.3351
PDL01	0.137846	0.010721	12.85697	0.0000
PDL02	-0.002841	0.001587	-1.789976	0.0774
PDL03	-0.005128	0.001625	-3.156107	0.0023

R-squared	0.992775	Mean dependent var	4532.488
Adjusted R-squared	0.992489	S.D. dependent var	2178.082
S.E. of regression	188.7615	Akaike info criterion	13.36755
Sum squared resid	2707949.	Schwarz criterion	13.48665
Log likelihood	-530.7021	F-statistic	3480.793
Durbin-Watson stat	0.387695	Prob(F-statistic)	0.000000

Lag Distribution of X	i	Coefficient	Std. Error	T-Statistic
	0	0.06717	0.01523	4.41119
	1	0.10022	0.00511	19.5968
	2	0.12302	0.00541	22.7408
	3	0.13556	0.00941	14.4013
	4	0.13785	0.01072	12.8570
	5	0.12988	0.00908	14.3058
	6	0.11165	0.00534	20.9195
	7	0.08318	0.00735	11.3228
	8	0.04444	0.01797	2.47277
Sum of Lags		0.93296	0.01147	81.3345

Our estimates of γ_1 and γ_2 will differ from the text Table 15.3 since EViews uses a formula for representing the pattern of lag weights (β_i) that differs slightly from equation (15.2.8). For PDL models with even lag length (*n*), the EViews formula calculates the lag distance from the center lag (*n*/2) – rather than from zero as in the text – as follows:

$$\beta_i = \gamma_0 + \gamma_1(i - n/2) + \gamma_2(i - n/2)^2$$

Note: This formulation implies that when $i = n/2$, $\beta_{n/2} = \gamma_0$, whereas in the text $\beta_0 = \gamma_0$. In our current capital expenditure application, $n = 8$ and so we expect $\beta_4 = \gamma_0$ as it does, noting the EViews coefficient on PDL01 equals the coefficient at lag 4 which in turn equals 0.138. Note however that despite the difference in our γ estimates, the coefficients of primary interest, the lag weights (β_i), have precisely the same numerical values, standard errors, and t-statistics as those presented in Table 15.4.

EViews provides a plot of the lag weights (β_i) against the lag i which, other than being rotated clockwise 90 degrees, matches the lag weights marked degree 2 in Figure 15.3.

15.3   Selection of the Length of the Finite Lag

In order to select the appropriate lag length (n) for a distributed lag model, we make our first use of the Akaike and Schwarz criteria reported under the coefficient table after every EViews least squares estimation. Our objective is to minimize these criteria, each of which is a function of the sum of squared errors, $\sum e^2$. Note however that each of these criteria includes a second term, a degrees of freedom penalty for including additional lag weights. EViews displays the two criteria in the section of regression statistics that follows the table of estimation results. Our strategy is to run models of increasing lag length (n) and select the lag length that minimizes the Akaike and Schwarz criteria.

R-squared	0.992775	Mean dependent var	4532.488
Adjusted R-squared	0.992489	S.D. dependent var	2178.082
S.E. of regression	188.7615	Akaike info criterion	13.36755
Sum squared resid	2707949.	Schwarz criterion	13.48665
Log likelihood	-530.7021	F-statistic	3480.793
Durbin-Watson stat	0.387695	Prob(F-statistic)	0.000000

15.4   An Illustration of the ARDL Model

In this section we estimate the autoregressive distributed lag ARDL(1,1) model of the capital expenditures equation (15.5.1) and plot the lag weights using an EViews program to partially replicate Figure 15.5. In the EViews command window enter

EQUATION EQ15_5_1.LS C X X(-1) Y(-1)

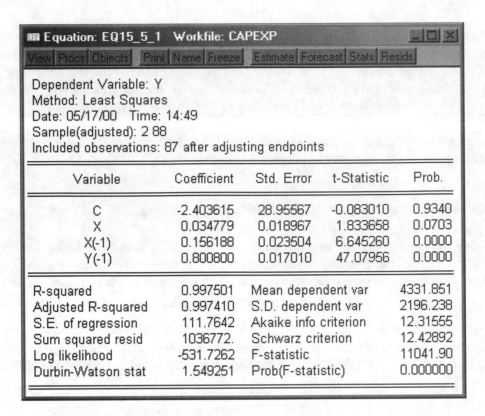

With reference to equation (15.5.1) in the text, note that $C(1) = \mu$, $C(2) = \beta_0$, the coefficient on X, $C(3) = \beta_1$, the coefficient on X(-1), and $C(4) = \gamma_1$, the coefficient on Y(-1). Note that the coefficients on lagged appropriations, X(-1), and lagged capital expenditures, Y(-1), are strongly statistically significant and positive. To plot the lags from this problem, we use the EViews program **ARDL11** available for download from the textbook website. This program will plot the first eight lag weights from the most recently estimated ARDL(1,1) equation. Open the program, click on **Run**, and then click **OK**.

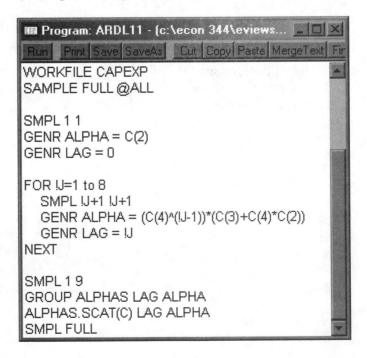

After freezing the group as a graph named **fig15_5** and adding titles we have the following partial replication of Figure 15.5 in the text.

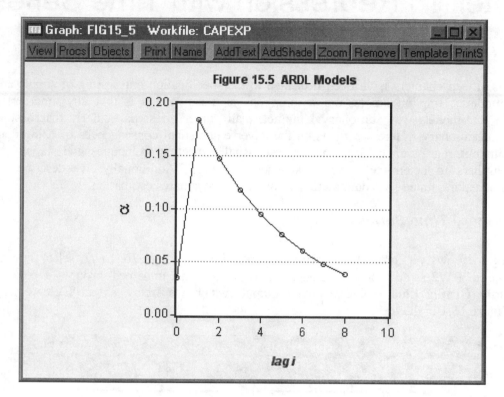

Chapter 16 Regression with Time Series Data

The previous fifteen chapters have been dedicated to the specification and testing of simple and multiple regression models. Implicit among our assumptions in those models is that any time series data we employed in our models was stationary. In fact, many time series, particularly macroeconomic time series, are nonstationary. Here we focus on the adverse statistical consequences of using nonstationary time series in our regression models and suggest visual inspection techniques and statistical tests that permit researchers to determine if series are nonstationary. Additionally, we describe differencing techniques for making time series data stationary prior to least squares estimation.

16.1 Stationary Time Series

To produce an EViews version of Figure 16.1, we open the workfile *fig16_1.wf1*, select the variables S1, S2, RW1, and RW2, and open a group. Next, from the unnamed group's toolbar we select **View/Multiple Graphs/Line**. The resulting output, which we freeze as an EViews graph object, replicates Figure 16.1 in the text:

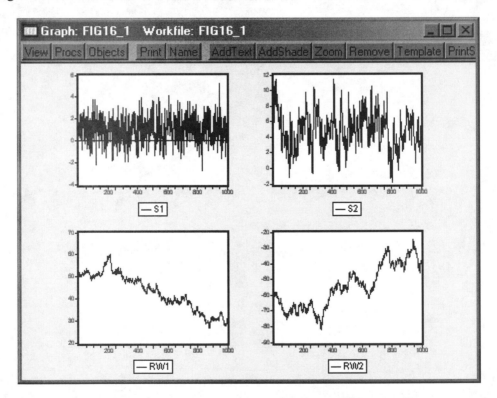

To produce Figure 16.2 in EViews, open the workfile *fig16_2.wf1*, select the variables INFLATION, LEADING_INDIC, PCE, PDI, and PRIME_RATE and open a group. Next, from the unnamed group's toolbar we select **View/Multiple Graphs/Line**. The resulting output, which we freeze as an EViews graph object, reproduces Figure 16.2 in the text:

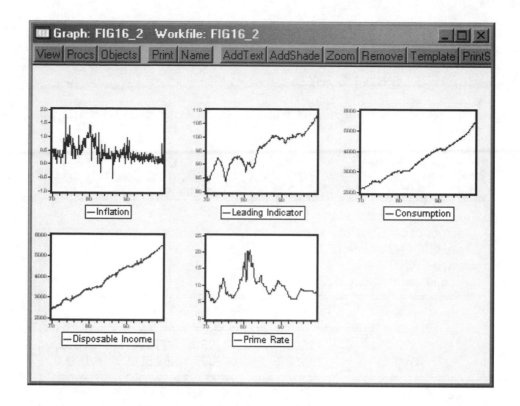

16.2 Spurious Regressions

Next, we use EViews graphing capabilities to create a scatterplot of RW1 against RW2 as shown below:

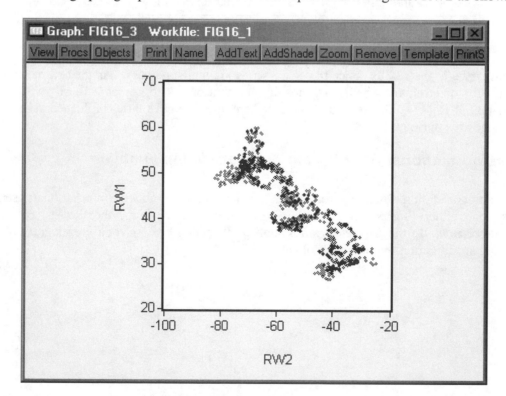

This simple scatterplot clearly reveals an inverse relationship between RW1 and RW2. Moreover, a simple regression of RW1 on RW2, conducted in the EViews command window by the command

EQUATION TABLE16_1.LS RW1 C RW2

shows that the model has a reasonably good fit with $R^2 = 0.75$. Our regression results match those found in Table 16.1 in the text:

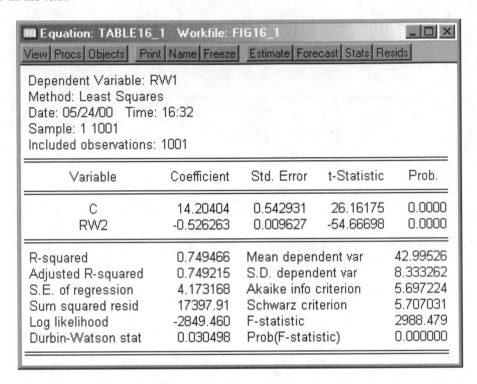

Equation: TABLE16_1 Workfile: FIG16_1

View | Procs | Objects | Print | Name | Freeze | Estimate | Forecast | Stats | Resids

Dependent Variable: RW1
Method: Least Squares
Date: 05/24/00   Time: 16:32
Sample: 1 1001
Included observations: 1001

Variable	Coefficient	Std. Error	t-Statistic	Prob.
C	14.20404	0.542931	26.16175	0.0000
RW2	-0.526263	0.009627	-54.66698	0.0000

R-squared	0.749466	Mean dependent var		42.99526
Adjusted R-squared	0.749215	S.D. dependent var		8.333262
S.E. of regression	4.173168	Akaike info criterion		5.697224
Sum squared resid	17397.91	Schwarz criterion		5.707031
Log likelihood	-2849.460	F-statistic		2988.479
Durbin-Watson stat	0.030498	Prob(F-statistic)		0.000000

This regression model is referred to as a spurious regression, and, as the text indicates, we should not have any confidence in the results, since these two series are non-stationary. As the text indicates, a quick rule of thumb for determining whether our results are spurious is to compare the R^2 with the Durbin-Watson statistic. If $R^2 > DW$, as is clearly the case here, then we have little confidence in our results and suspect that they are spurious.

16.3 Checking Stationarity Using the Autocorrelation Function

To plot the autocorrelation functions for the stationary series S2 and the nonstationary series RW1, double-click on either series in workfile *fig16_1.wf1* and from the series toolbar, select **View/Correlogram....** In the **Correlogram Specification** dialog box, select a correlogram of the **Level** of S2, and a lag specification that includes **10** lags of S2:

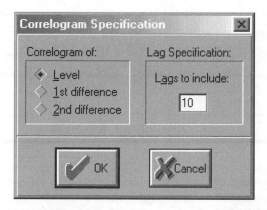

Click **OK** to obtain the correlogram shown in Table 16.2 in the text.

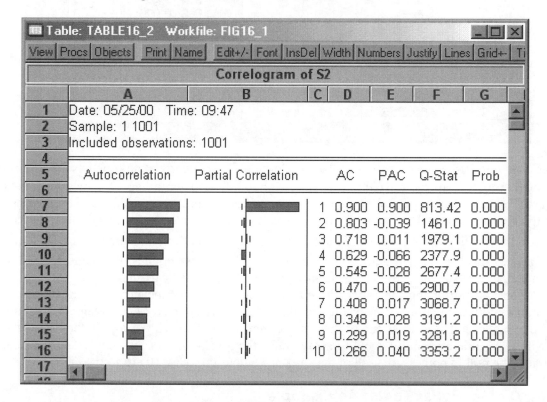

Note that EViews provides us with the partial autocorrelation function (PAC) as well as the autocorrelation function (AC). We will ignore the partial autocorrelation function here. As explained in the text, the dotted lines found in the correlogram are statistical significance bounds. Any autocorrelation that exceeds these bounds either positively or negatively is statistically significant. For the AC of S2, the first ten lags are statistically significant. We follow the same procedure to produce Table 16.3, the correlogram for the nonstationary series RW1:

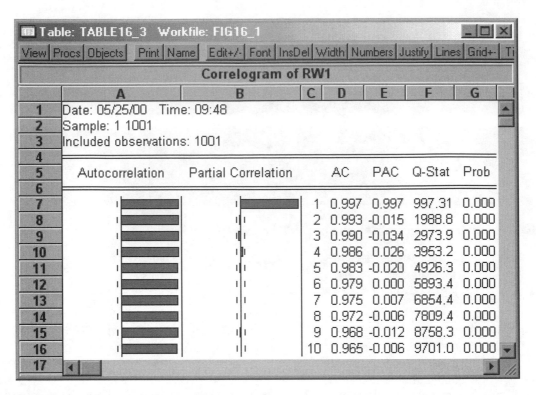

Note that over our 10-lag specification of the correlogram, the autocorrelation function never dies out and the estimated autocorrelations, ρ_s, fall only slightly from 0.997 to 0.965 at lag 10, indicating a persistently high degree of correlation of RW1 with its past values. These estimated autocorrelations are all statistically significant as they lie well beyond the two standard error bounds that EViews uses to approximate the confidence interval stated in the text. These bounds are computed as $\pm 2/\sqrt{T}$, where T is the sample size. If an estimated autocorrelation lies outside of these bounds, it is considered statistically significant at the 5% level. We can further confirm the statistical significance of the estimated autocorrelations by examining the Ljung-Box Q-statistics and their associated p-values. The Q-statistic tests the null hypothesis that all of the estimated autocorrelations up to some given lag are zero against the alternative hypothesis that at least one of them is non-zero. For example, for lag 10, the Q-statistic equals 9701.0 with a p-value essentially equal to zero. Since the p-value is less than our 5% significance level, we can reject the null hypothesis that all of the autocorrelations up to lag 10 are zero.

16.4 The Dickey-Fuller Tests: An Example

For determining stationarity, a more sophisticated alternative to the visual inspection of the ACF correlogram is the unit root test. To conduct this test, double-click on the personal consumption expenditure (PCE) series in the *fig16_2.wf1* workfile and select **View/Unit Root Test...** from the series toolbar. In the unit root test dialog box specify an **Augmented Dickey-Fuller** test type, test for a unit root in the **Level** of PCE, include an **Intercept** with no trend, enter **0** for the number of lagged difference terms, and click **OK**.

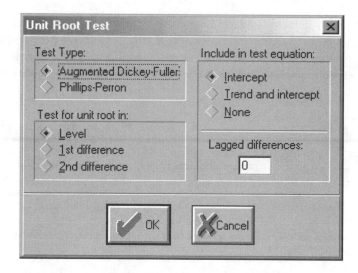

Our results match equation (16.4.10a) in the text:

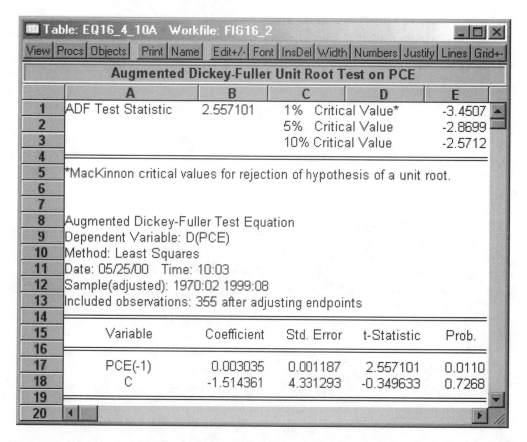

Note that the Augmented Dickey-Fuller (ADF) critical values reported by EViews match those given in row 2 of Table 16.4 in the chapter for the ADF model including the intercept. The ADF test statistic, *tau*, is 2.557, which is shown as the *t*-statistic on the lag of personal consumption expenditures, PCE(-1), in the regression output. Thus *tau* is not significantly negative since it is positive and hence greater than the 10% critical value of -2.57 and we fail to reject the null hypothesis of a unit root in the personal consumption expenditure series.

To conduct the ADF test with trend, select **View/Unit Root Test...** from the personal consumption expenditure (PCE) series toolbar. In the unit root test dialog box specify an **Augmented Dickey-Fuller** test type, test for a unit root in the **Level** of PCE, check **Trend and Intercept**, enter **0** for the number of lagged difference terms, and click **OK**. Our results agree with equation (16.4.10b) in the text:

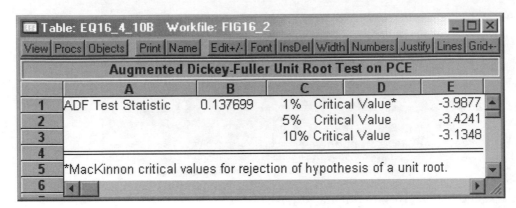

For convenience, the EViews output presented above has been truncated. Using the scroll bar to scroll down through the output, we find the actual least squares output for equation (16.4.10b) in the text, including the trend term, t. Note that the ADF critical values match those presented in Table 16.4 in the text in row 3 for the model with trend, t. The ADF test statistic, tau, is once again not significantly negative enough to reject the null hypothesis of a unit root.

Finally, we consider an ADF test with two lagged difference terms, ΔPCE_{t-1} and ΔPCE_{t-2}. Once again, we select **View/Unit Root Test...** from the personal consumption expenditure (PCE) series toolbar. In the unit root test dialog box we specify an **Augmented Dickey-Fuller** test type, test for a unit root in the **Level** of PCE, check **Intercept**, enter **2** for the number of lagged difference terms, and click **OK**. Our results replicate with equation (16.4.10c) in the text:

Table: EQ16_4_10C   Workfile: FIG16_2

View | Procs | Objects | Print | Name | Edit+/- | Font | InsDel | Width | Numbers | Justify | Lines | Grid+-

Augmented Dickey-Fuller Unit Root Test on PCE

	A	B	C	D	E
1	ADF Test Statistic	3.306833	1% Critical Value*		-3.4508
2			5% Critical Value		-2.8699
3			10% Critical Value		-2.5712
4					
5	*MacKinnon critical values for rejection of hypothesis of a unit root.				
6					

The EViews MacKinnon critical values are the same as the critical values reported in row 2 of Table 16.4 in the text for the model with intercept only. Once again, the ADF test statistic, $tau = 3.31$, is positive and therefore we fail to reject the null hypothesis of a unit root.

We turn now to an investigation of the stationarity of the first difference of the personal consumption expenditure series $\Delta PCE_t = PCE_t - PCE_{t-1}$. To construct this series, enter the following command into the EViews command window

GENR DPCE = D(PCE)

where D( ) is the EViews difference operator. Double-click on this series in the workfile and select **View/Line Graph** to create Figure 16.4 in the text.

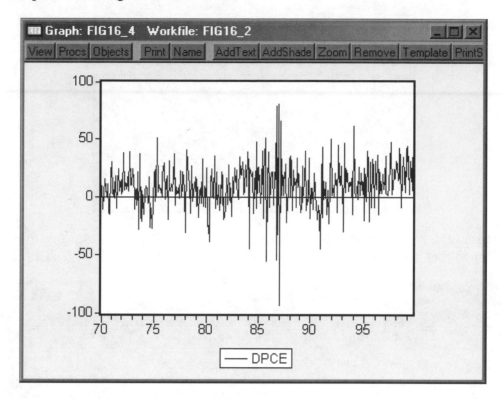

We click **View/Correlogram...** and select a lag length of 10 to examine the correlogram of DPCE and find small and statistically insignificant autocorrclations at lags two through 10 with a small and statistically significant autocorrelation at lag 1. In time series terminology we say the autocorrelation function of the first difference of personal consumption expenditures "cuts off" after the first lag. Note that EViews allows us to examine the correlogram of the first and second differences of any series without first generating the differenced series itself by simply specifying the difference level in the **Correlogram Specification** dialog box. In the present application we checked **Level** since we had generated the new variable DPCE, the first difference of PCE. Had we selected PCE from the workfile, we would have checked **1ˢᵗ diference** in the **Correlogram Specification** dialog box and achieved the same results.

To replicate equation (16.4.11), the ADF test equation for DPCE, double-click on DPCE in the workfile and select **View/Correlogram...** from the series toolbar. Specify the ADF test equation in the **Level**, check **None** under **Include in test equation**, and set the lagged differences to **0**.

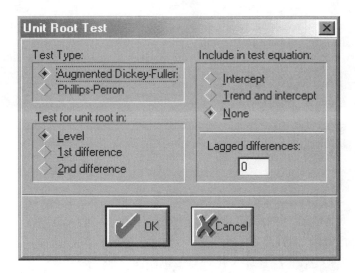

The ADF test statistic, *tau* = -18.668, is significantly negative in this case, allowing us to reject the null hypothesis of a unit root in the first difference of personal consumption expenditures, DPCE.

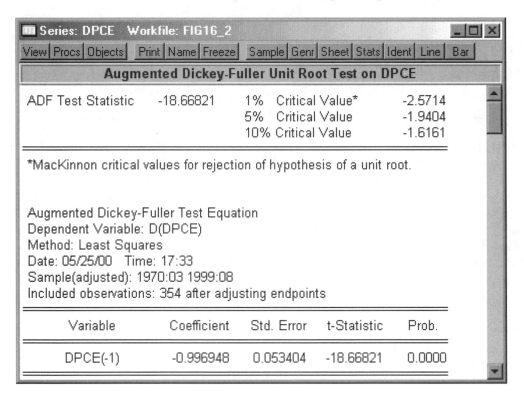

16.5 An Example of a Cointegration Test

To conduct the test for cointegration between consumption PCE and disposable income PDI we apply an Augmented Dickey-Fuller test to the residuals ε_t from a least squares estimation of equation (16.5.2). Enter the following commands into the EViews command window

```
EQUATION EQ16_5_2.LS PCE C PDI          Estimates equation (16.5.2)
GENR E = RESID                          Generates the residual series E
```

To apply the Augmented Dickey-Fuller (ADF) test to the residuals ε_t, in the workfile we double-click on the series E and select **View/Unit Root Test....** Specify the test type as Augmented Dickey-Fuller, test for a unit root in the Level of ε_t, check Intercept to include an intercept in the ADF test equation, and finally enter 0 to exclude lagged differences.

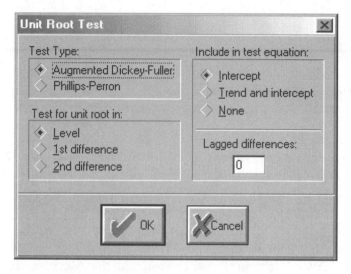

Our ADF cointegration test results are

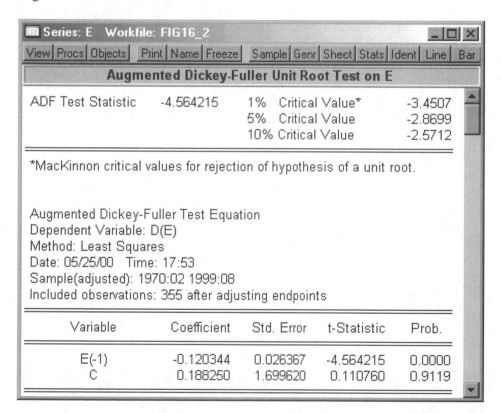

The Augmented Dickey-Fuller (ADF) test statistic *tau* = -4.564, which is significantly more negative than even the 1% critical value of −3.451 so we reject the null hypothesis of a unit root in the ε_t, providing statistical evidence that PCE and PDI are cointegrated. As a result of this cointegration, a simple linear regression of PCE on PDI constitutes a long-run equilibrium relationship.

Chapter 17 Pooling Time Series and Cross-Sectional Data

Researchers may have access to time series and cross section data, both of which are relevant to a particular empirical problem. For example, we may have data on the investment decisions of several firms for various years. Alternatively, a study of the determinants of economic growth may rely on data for a variety of developing and industrialized nations over many decades. Chapter 17 introduces models for combining such time series and cross-sectional data and describes situations in which these methods are appropriate.

17.1 Estimating Separate Equations

To estimate separate investment equations for GE and Westinghouse, we open the workfile *invest1.wf1*, click on **Quick/Estimate Equation**, and enter equation (17.2.3) by typing **INVG C VG KG** in the equation specification dialog box. After estimating equation (17.2.3), we save the residuals by typing **GENR EG = RESID** into the EViews command window. Repeat this procedure for the Westinghouse equation: **INVW C VW KW**. Alternatively, we can estimate the investment equations directly from the command window by typing the following series of commands:

EQUATION EQG_LS.LS INVG C VG KG	**Estimates the GE investment equation**
GENR EG = RESID	**Saves the GE residuals (EG)**
EQUATION EQW_LS.LS INVW C VW KW	**Estimates the Westinghouse equation**
GENR EW = RESID	**Saves the Westinghouse residuals (EW)**

Our results match the least squares (LS) results found in Table 17.1 in the text, shown here for GE only:

```
┌─ Equation: EQG_LS   Workfile: INVEST1 ─────────── _□X ─┐
│ View│Procs│Objects│  Print│Name│Freeze│ Estimate│Forecast│Stats│Resids│
├────────────────────────────────────────────────────┤
│ Dependent Variable: INVG                            │
│ Method: Least Squares                               │
│ Date: 11/08/99   Time: 10:37                        │
│ Sample: 1 20                                        │
│ Included observations: 20                           │
│                                                     │
│   Variable    Coefficient  Std. Error  t-Statistic   Prob. │
│                                                     │
│      C         -9.956306    31.37425   -0.317340   0.7548 │
│     VG          0.026551     0.015566   1.705705   0.1063 │
│     KG          0.151694     0.025704   5.901548   0.0000 │
│                                                     │
│ R-squared           0.705307  Mean dependent var   102.2900 │
│ Adjusted R-squared  0.670637  S.D. dependent var   48.58450 │
│ S.E. of regression  27.88272  Akaike info criterion 9.631373 │
│ Sum squared resid   13216.59  Schwarz criterion     9.780733 │
│ Log likelihood     -93.31373  F-statistic          20.34355 │
│ Durbin-Watson stat  1.072099  Prob(F-statistic)     0.000031 │
└─────────────────────────────────────────────────────┘
```

17.2 Separate or Joint Estimation

To carry out the statistical test of the hypothesis that there is zero correlation between the error terms from the two separately estimated equations, we must construct the test statistic $\lambda = T r^2_{GW}$, where r^2_{GW} is the r^2 from a simple regression of EG on EW. To calculate λ, enter the following commands into the EViews command window:

```
EQUATION  EQ_R2GW.LS EG EW          Estimates equation EQ_R2GW
SCALAR LAMBDA = @REGOBS*@R2          Calculates λ = Tr²GW
SCALAR CHICRIT = @QCHISQ(.95,1)      Calculates the χ² critical value
```

where @REGOBS is the number of regression observations (T=20) and @R2 is the r^2 (r^2_{GW} = 0.5314) from the regression of EG on EW. Since λ = 10.628, which is greater than the χ^2 critical value of 3.84, we reject the null hypothesis H_0: σ_{GW} = 0, and find evidence of the presence of contemporaneously correlated error terms. We can place the results of this test in a results vector with the following commands:

```
EQUATION  EQ_R2GW.LS EG EW          Estimates equation EQ_R2GW
COEF(3) LAMBDACHI                    Creates a storage vector
LAMBDACHI(1) = @REGOBS*@R2           Calculates λ = Tr²GW
LAMBDACHI(2) = @QCHISQ(.95,1)        Calculates the χ² critical value
```

We freeze our results vector LAMBDACHI to create a table named R17_1 in the workfile as follows:

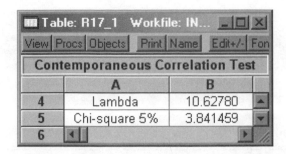

To estimate the Seemingly Unrelated Regression (SUR) model of equation (17.2.2), we create a pool object in EViews. Select **Object/New Object** from the EViews menubar, select the pool object type, enter a name for the object (**POOL_SUR**), and click **OK**.

Next, we enter cross-section identifiers for our model. We are working with N=2 cross-section components, G = GE and W = Westinghouse, and our workfile variables INV, V, and K, are tagged with these letters as suffixes so we enter

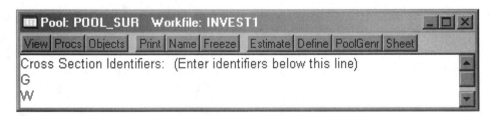

To estimate the SUR model, equation (17.2.2), click on **Estimate** on the Pool's toolbar to bring up the **Pooled Estimation** dialog box.

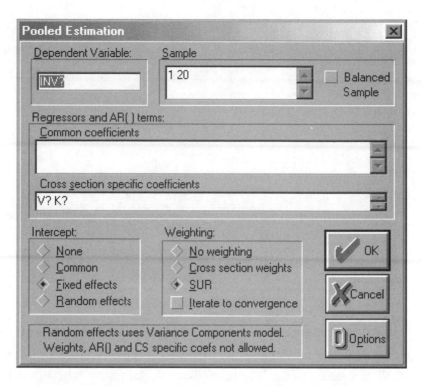

When estimating a model with pooled cross section and time series data, EViews gives us many estimation options. First, note that we refer to the variables INVG and INVW as INV?, where the **?** acts as a placeholder or wildcard for the cross-section identifiers we entered when we created the pool object. Second, note that we enter the variables V? and K? as **cross section specific coefficients**. Examine equation (17.2.2) once again. Note that the β's do not vary through time, but are specific to each cross section unit (ie, each firm i = G,W). We know this is the case because the β's have i subscripts but no t subscripts. The intercept is treated as a **fixed effects** intercept that varies across firms. Finally, under "Weighting", we check **SUR** to estimate the SUR model.

Our results match those found in Table 17.1 in the text:

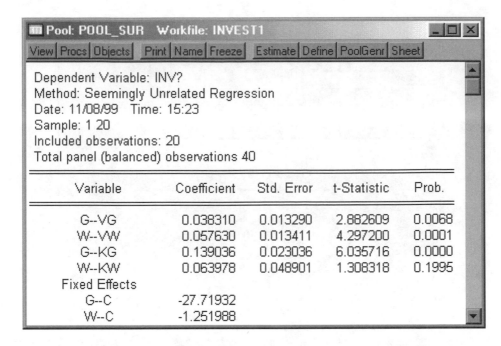

In EViews terminology, G--VG is the response coefficient for stock market value (V) that is specific to the GE cross section; W is specific to the Westinghouse cross section. Under **Fixed Effects**, G--C is the GE intercept and W--C is the Westinghouse intercept.

17.3 A Dummy Variable Specification

In this section, we use the investment data found in the workfile ***invest2.wf1*** to illustrate and compare the estimation of a dummy variable or "fixed effects" model, and an error components or "random effects" model. Note that EViews uses the terms "fixed effects" and "random effects" for these models. At issue is whether we should allow the cross sectional intercepts to be constants or random variables that represent differences in firm behavior. To estimate the fixed effects model in equation (17.3.4), we select **Object/New Object** from the EViews menubar and select pool. We name this pool EQ17_3_4U, where the "U" stands for the unrestricted version of equation (17.3.4). We enter the cross section identifiers for firms: **GM USX GE CH AR IBM UO WE GY DM**. Next, we click on **Estimate** on the Pool's toolbar. We use the EViews placeholder character "?" to enter our dependent variable **INV?**. Note that whereas in the SUR model we allowed the slope and intercept coefficients to vary across firms, in the fixed effects model we only allow the intercept to vary across firms. Consequently, we enter the variables **V?** and **K?** in the common coefficients field of the pooled estimation dialog box. We check **Fixed Effects** in the intercept field and **No weighting** under the Weighting field.

Our results match Table 17.2 in the text:

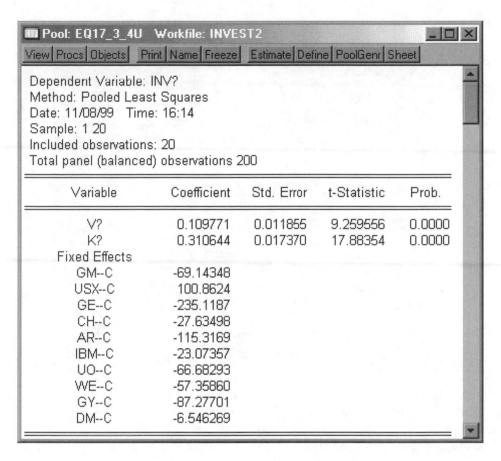

To conduct the F test for the hypothesis that the intercepts are equal across all cross section units represented by the coefficient restrictions in equation (17.3.5), we must save the sum of squared residuals from this unrestricted model. We enter the following command in the EViews command window:

```
SCALAR SSE_U = EQ17_3_4U.@SSR
```

Next, we need to restrict the model by specifying that all of the firm intercepts are equal, and then calculate the sum of squared residuals from this restricted model. We create a new pool object with the same cross section identifiers as EQ17_3_4U and name it EQ17_3_4R, where the "R" stands for restricted. Click **Estimate** from the Pool's toolbar and fill out the Pooled Estimation dialog box as follows:

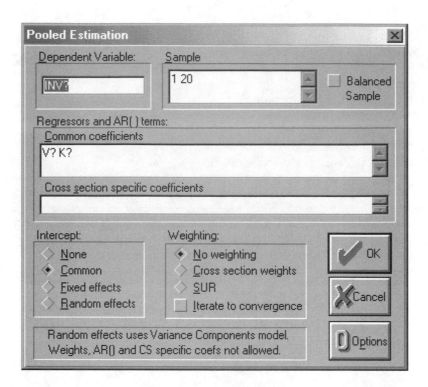

Note that we change our specification to include a **common** intercept in the restricted model and we select **no weighting** instead of SUR. We will not report the results of the restricted model here. To construct the F statistic to test the hypothesis in equation (17.3.5) of the text, enter the following commands into the EViews command window:

SCALAR SSE_R = EQ17_3_4R.@SSR   Saves SSE_R
SCALAR F = ((SSE_R - SSE_U)/9)/(SSE_U/(200 - 12))   Calculates F stat
SCALAR FCRIT = @QFDIST(.95,9,188)   Calculates F crit

Since the F statistic under the null hypothesis that the intercepts are equal across firms, 48.99, is less than the critical $F_{(.05,9,188)} = 1.93$, we reject the null hypothesis of a common intercept in our model. Double-click on the F and FCRIT scalars in the workfile to view their values in the bottom left-hand corner of the EViews main window:

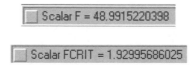

Scalar F = 48.9915220398

Scalar FCRIT = 1.92995686025

17.4 An Error Components Model

Alternatively, we might consider the cross sectional intercepts to be random variables related to differences in individual firm behavior. To estimate such a "random effects" model in EViews, we create another pool object and name it EQ17_4_5. We enter the same cross section identifiers as we did for the fixed effects model and click on **Estimate**. We need only change our intercept specification to "Random Effects" in the Pooled Estimation dialog box:

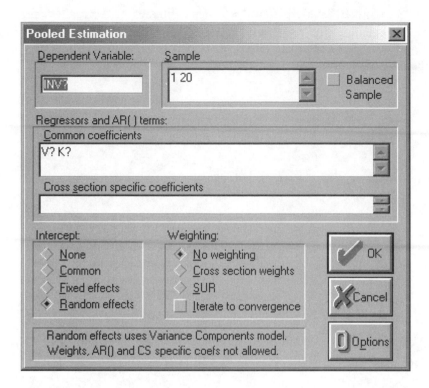

Our results replicate equation (17.4.5) in the text:

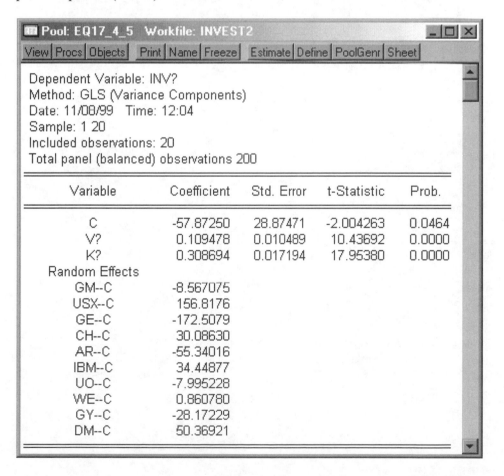

Under the heading "Random Effects", EViews provides estimates of the random firm-specific intercepts, β_{1i}. Note that we can calculate the firm specific errors, μ_i, from the formula given in equation (17.4.2) and our estimate of the population mean intercept, which is listed as the intercept coefficient C in the upper portion of the EViews output and equals -57.873.

Chapter 18: Qualitative and Limited Dependent Variable Models

For many empirical applications, our dependent variable is not continuous but rather binary. For example, in election years we are curious about the determinants of voting for Democrats or Republicans. Real estate agents and county planning departments are interested in the determinants of home ownership. Environmental groups want to know how decisions to recycle are formed. All of these examples have in common the binary nature of their dependent variables. People either recycle or they don't, they vote Democrat or Republican (don't vote Democrat), they own a home, or they rent. Here we consider models that are specifically designed to handle such binary choice applications.

18.1 An Example

Here we illustrate the application of the Probit model by considering a discrete choice model of the determinants of public transportation. We open the workfile *transport.wf1* and click on **Quick/Estimate Equation**. Under **Estimation Settings: Method**, click on the down arrow, and select **BINARY**, the EViews maximum likelihood estimator for qualitative dependent variable models.

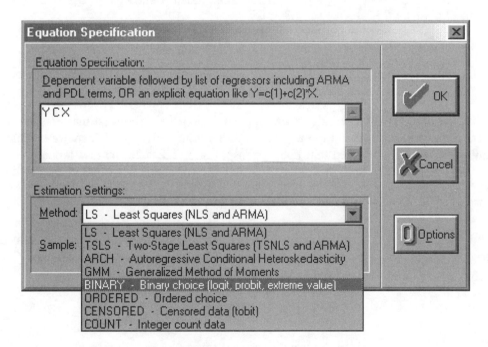

To run the probit model with an intercept and X, the difference between bus time and travel time, we specify the model as **Y C X**. Alternatively, we can type the command **BINARY(D=N) Y C X** in the EViews command window. Our estimation results are:

```
■■ Equation: R18_1  Workfile: TRANSPORT                    _ |□| x|
View| Procs| Objects|  Print | Name| Freeze|  Estimate| Forecast| Stats| Resids|

Dependent Variable: Y
Method: ML - Binary Probit
Date: 10/18/99   Time: 16:04
Sample: 1 21
Included observations: 21
Convergence achieved after 4 iterations
Covariance matrix computed using second derivatives

    Variable      Coefficient    Std. Error    z-Statistic      Prob.

        C          -0.064434      0.399239     -0.161391       0.8718
        X           0.029999      0.010286      2.916350       0.0035

Mean dependent var      0.476190    S.D. dependent var        0.511766
S.E. of regression      0.310890    Akaike info criterion     0.777634
Sum squared resid       1.836405    Schwarz criterion         0.877112
Log likelihood         -6.165158    Hannan-Quinn criter.      0.799223
Restr. log likelihood -14.53227     Avg. log likelihood      -0.293579
LR statistic (1 df)    16.73423     McFadden R-squared        0.575761
Probability(LR stat)   4.30E-05

Obs with Dep=0             11        Total obs                     21
Obs with Dep=1            10
```

Consistent with the standard normal distribution from which the Probit estimator is derived, note that EViews reports the *z*-statistic rather than a *t*-statistic for each coefficient. Next, we calculate the change in the probability of auto travel given that public transportation takes 20 minutes longer than car travel, as reported in result (R18.2) in the text. We enter the following command in the command window:

SCALAR DPDX20 = @DNORM(C(1) + C(2)*20)*C(2),

where @DNORM is EViews' standard normal probability density function *f(z)* given immediately above equation (18.2.8) in the text.   In the workfile, we double-click on the scalar ▦ dpdx_20 to view the result in the bottom left-hand corner of the EViews main window:

```
▢ Scalar DPDX_20 = 0.0103689956252
```

To calculate the estimated probability that an individual for whom public transportation takes 30 minutes longer than driving (x = 30) will choose to drive, we enter the following command:

SCALAR Y30 = 1-@CNORM(-(C(1) + C(2)*30))

where @CNORM is EViews' standard normal cumulative distribution function. We double-click on the scalar ▦ y30 to view the result of this calculation, which replicates result (R18.3):

```
▢ Scalar Y30 = 0.798291902937
```

Chapter 19 Obtaining Economic Data from the Internet

All of the work we've presented in previous chapters is to help you develop, estimate, and interpret economic relationships. While important (and fun!) in and of itself, economic research usually culminates in a written report. No one wants to wade through pages of EViews output; you must present your model, estimation results, and interpretations in a format readable to your audience. EViews graphs and equation output is easily pasted into documents. The pasting of graphs is discussed in Chapter 1.7.3 of this manual.

In this chapter, we take you to the Internet and show how easy it can be to obtain data for your research. Getting data for economic research is much easier today than it was years ago. Before the Internet, hours would be spent in libraries, looking for and copying down data by hand. Now, we have access to wonderful sources of data right at our fingertips. You are encouraged to visit the sites listed in *UE/2*, as well as doing a search from within your browser. Here, we show how to download data from two different websites and get it into an Excel spreadsheet. Once the data are in the spreadsheet, importing them into EViews is straightforward, as discussed in Chapter 1.3 of this manual.

We are interested in estimating a simple model of GDP as a function of personal consumption.

$$Y_t = \beta_1 + \beta_2 C_t + e_t$$

(Of course, we know the problems associated with this model, right?)

19.1 Obtaining Data from Economagic

- Open your Internet browser. (Here, we show using Netscape Communicator.)
- On the Location or Address bar, type **http://www.economagic.com**. (Actually, the http:// is not needed.)

- Follow the instructions as shown in the next series of pictures. (Lines separate each step.)

- ○ <u>Internal Revenue Service</u>: Tax Collections
- ○ **Department of Commerce**
  - ■ <u>BEA: National Accounts (GDP)</u>: 137 series
  - ■ <u>BEA: Gross State Product (GSP)</u>: 120 series
  - ■ <u>BEA: State Personal Income, Per Capita, and Population</u>: 177 series
  - ■ <u>Business Cycle Indicators</u>: Not updated, but popular
- ○ <u>Department of the Treasury</u>: US Public Debt
- ○ **<u>Department of Energy: Monthly Energy</u>**

> Scroll down and click on this link.

Gross Domestic Product

```
Y         Gross domestic product
C      Personal consumption expenditu
          Durable goods
```

> Choose this data series.

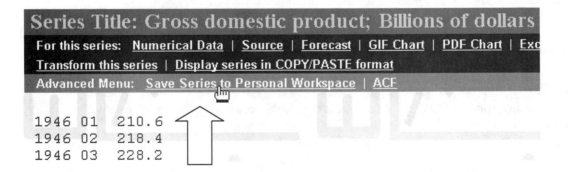

```
Series Title: Gross domestic product; Billions of dollars
For this series:  Numerical Data | Source | Forecast | GIF Chart | PDF Chart | Exc
Transform this series | Display series in COPY/PASTE format
Advanced Menu:  Save Series to Personal Workspace | ACF

1946 01   210.6
1946 02   218.4
1946 03   228.2
```

- At this point, a new screen shows that this series has been put into your workspace. Hit the Back button on your browser until you are back to the data links. Choose the next data file.

Browse NIPA Data of the Bur

Gross Domestic Product

```
Y        Gross domestic product
C     Personal consumption expenditures
            Durable goods
            Nondurable goods
            Services
```

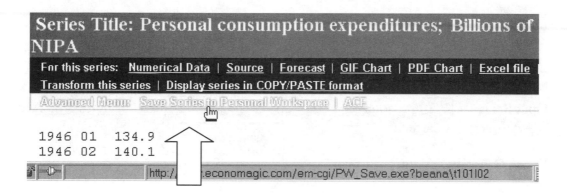

Series Title: Personal consumption expenditures; Billions of NIPA

For this series: **Numerical Data** | **Source** | **Forecast** | **GIF Chart** | **PDF Chart** | **Excel file**
Transform this series | **Display series in COPY/PASTE format**
Advanced Menu: Save Series to Personal Workspace | ACE

```
1946 01   134.9
1946 02   140.1
```

http://   .economagic.com/em-cgi/PW_Save.exe?beana\t101l02

Current Personal Workspace

If you wish, choose one or two series for transformations.

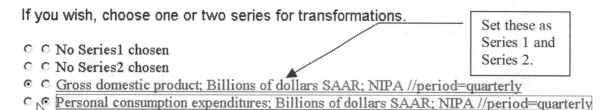

- ○ ○ No Series1 chosen
- ○ ○ No Series2 chosen
- ⦿ ○ Gross domestic product; Billions of dollars SAAR; NIPA //period=quarterly
- ○ ⦿ Personal consumption expenditures; Billions of dollars SAAR; NIPA //period=quarterly

Set these as
Series 1 and
Series 2.

Copy Multiple Series to One Excel File, or Display in Copy & Paste Format

[Click here to start]

Copy several series to a spreadsheet

Input Series # [1]   Gross domestic product; Billions of dollars SAAR; NIPA//period=quarterly

Input Series # [2]   Personal consumption expenditures; Billions of dollars SAAR; NIPA//period=quarterly

Change these
to "1" and "2".

Excel ⊙   Copy and Paste format ○

Use number 1 for the first series, 2 for the second etc.. Use zero to series.

Please be patient with the creation of Excel files. This could take at seconds.

[Copy selected series]

Please find your 2 series in the excel file linked below.

Series #1: Gross domestic product; Billions of dollars SAAR; NIPA//period=quarterly
Series #2: Personal consumption expenditures; Billions of dollars SAAR; NIPA//period=quarterly

Click here for your data in an Excel file

At this point, you will download the files into Excel. Depending on your browser, Excel may open automatically and the data will appear, or you may be asked to save the data to disc. In any event, the data should appear as

	A	B	C	D	E	F	G
	144075012025212481.xls						
1	http://www.economagic.com/						
2	Series #1	Gross domestic product; Billions of dollars SAAR; NIPA					
3	Series #2	Personal consumption expenditures; Billions of dollars SAAR; NIPA					
4							
5				Series #1	Series #2		
6	Jan-1946	1946	1	210.6	134.9		
7	Apr-1946	1946	2	218.4	140.1		
8	Jul-1946	1946	3	228.2	148.9		
9	Oct-1946	1946	4	232	153.1		
10	Jan-1947	1947	1	237.5	156.5		
11	Apr-1947	1947	2	240.7	160.5		
12	Jul-1947	1947	3	244.9	164		
13	Oct-1947	1947	4	254.7	168.2		
14	Jan-1948	1948	1	260.8	170.9		

You should immediately **Save As** an Excel workbook for further use.

For other uses of Excel in econometrics, see *Using Excel for Undergraduate Econometrics, 2ⁿᵈ Edition*, by Karen Gutermuth and R. Carter Hill (John Wiley and Sons, Inc., 2001). The present chapter is taken from that book.

19.2 Obtaining Data in Text Format

Not all websites offer options to download data in particular formats, such as Excel. But obtaining this data and importing into Excel is not difficult.

- Point your browser to http://www.csufresno.edu/Economics/econ_EDL.htm.
- Scroll down to United States and click on **productivity**.

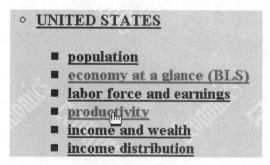

○ **UNITED STATES**

- **population**
- **economy at a glance (BLS)**
- **labor force and earnings**
- **productivity**
- **income and wealth**
- **income distribution**

- Under income and wealth, click on **per capita GDP**.

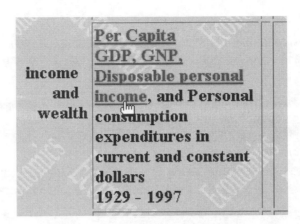

The following page appears.

```
No. 728. Selected Per Capita Income and Product Items
   in Current and Real (1992) Dollars

[In dollars. Based on Bureau of the Census estimated population incl
Forces abroad; based on quarterly averages]
```

Year	Current dollars		
	Gross domestic product	Disposable personal income	Personal consumption expend-tures
1960	2,913	2,008	1,838
1961	2,965	2,062	1,865
1962	3,136	2,151	1,948
1963	3,261	2,225	2,023
1964	3,455	2,384	2,144
1965	3,700	2,541	2,286

We are interested in obtaining the Gross domestic product data and the Personal consumption expenditures. You could copy and paste the data, but saving the entire file is much easier.

- From the menu, choose **File/Save As**.

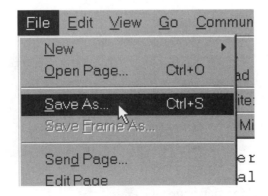

- Choose the proper folder in which to **Save in:**
- Rename the file *y_c.txt*.
- Click **OK**.

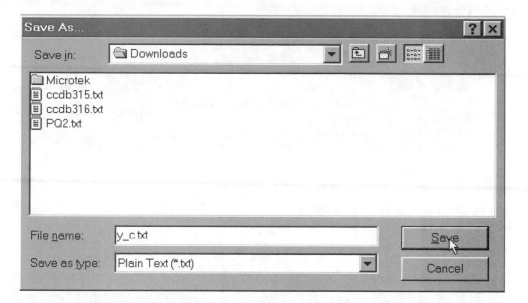

- Return to Excel.
- From the menu choose **File/Open** or click on the Open icon.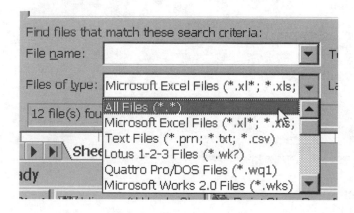
- Change the Files of type: to **All files (*.*)**.

- Locate the file you just downloaded, *y_c.txt*, click on it, and click **Open**.

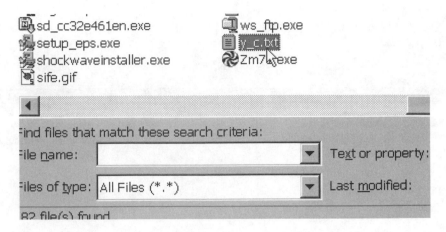

Excel's Import Wizard now starts.

- Choose the Original data type as **Delimited**.
- Start import at row: **10**
- Click **Next**.

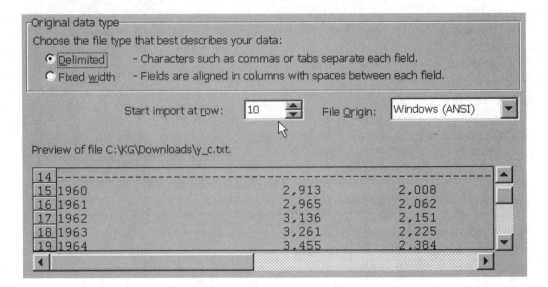

- Set the delimiter to **Space**.
- Click **Next**, and then **Finish**.

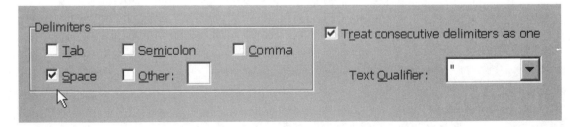

The data now appears as

	A	B	C	D	E	F	G
1		Year	Gross	Disposable	consumpti	popula-	
2		domestic	personal	expend-	tion		
3		product	income	tures	-1,000		
4							
5	--						
6	1960	2,913	2,008	1,838	180,760		
7	1961	2,965	2,062	1,865	183,742		
8	1962	3,136	2,151	1,948	186,590		
9	1963	3,261	2,225	2,023	189,300		
10	1964	3,455	2,384	2,144	191,927		
11	1965	3,700	2,541	2,286	194,347		✛
12	1966	4,007	2,715	2,451	196,599		
13	1967	4,194	2,877	2,563	198,752		
14	1968	4,536	3,096	2,789	200,745		
15	1969	4,845	3,297	2,982	202,736		

The labels need to be fixed, but then you're ready to go!

Excel's Import Wizard can import just about any data you have. You may have to play with it a bit, cleaning up particular cells, moving labels around, or deleting strange characters, but always remember to **Save As** an Excel workbook, and **Save** often after that!